BECOMING AGAIN

LESSONS FROM FALLING, FAILING, AND FINDING FAITH

"

YOU ARE NOT
YOUR MISTAKES.
YOU CAN REBUILD.
YOU CAN BECOME
AGAIN.

ABDULBASIT ABDUSALAM

ISBN 978-978-691-575-3

Cover design by Khalid Koiki
Edited by Aisha Animashaun

Author can be contacted via:
1abdulbasitabdusalam@gmail.com
Printed in Lagos, Nigeria

Published by:
Trustwell Ventures Nig. Ltd.
33, Durosimi Street, Onipanu, Opposite
Shomolu Central Mosque, Shomolu Lagos.
+234 802 396 3823, +234 903 125 2353
madinah1427@yahoo.co.uk
ummahtrust1434@gmail.com

Table of Contents

What People are Saying About the Book

Becoming Again is one of those rare books that speaks directly to the silent battles many young people carry. Abdulbasit writes with honesty that disarms you. His reflections on shame, failure, and self-discovery feel real because they are lived, not fictional.

What makes this book powerful is its clarity. It does not glamorise failure or minimise pain. Instead, it shows how resilience grows in quiet, disciplined moments and how faith steadies us when life bends unexpectedly.

As someone who has watched Abdulbasit embrace leadership, service, and growth over the years, from his pioneering role as the first Team Lead of the NGM Book Review Unit to his appointment as an Ambassador for Public Speaking and Writers Development, I recognise the maturity in these pages. This is a book for anyone who feels lost, delayed, or burdened by expectations. It reminds you that beginning again is not weakness. It is courage.

A deeply relatable and spiritually grounding read.

Engineer Nasir Giwa
Grand Mentor, Nasir Giwa Mentorship Platform.

There are books that simply tell a story, and there are books that guide a generation. Becoming Again is firmly the latter, an honest, unflinching exploration of what it means to fall, rise, and rebuild one's life with clarity and faith. Abdulbasit writes with a vulnerability that is both refreshing and required in a world where young people are taught to curate perfection while silently battling shame, doubt, and confusion. His reflections offer readers a courageous invitation to confront their failures not as endpoints but as raw material for transformation.

I first met Abdulbasit in 2023, and his story of persistence struck me deeply. Long before I knew the full arc of his journey, I recognised in him the rare combination of humility, grit, and curiosity that defines truly exceptional people. I was so moved by his resilience and hunger to grow that I offered him a position at Wennovation Hub even before he graduated. That same resilience pulses through every chapter of this book.

As someone who has spent years investing in founders and inspiring young people across Africa and beyond, I have seen up close how many are held back—not by lack of talent—but by the weight of past mistakes and the fear of beginning again. This book offers exactly what they need: permission to rise, framework to rebuild, and language to understand that failure is neither fatal nor final. Abdulbasit's message aligns powerfully with my own work in helping young Africans dare, dream, and even fail their way into success.

What sets Becoming Again apart is its spiritual depth. Abdulbasit shows that God often meets us most clearly in the aftermath of our missteps, guiding us toward discipline, accountability, and renewed purpose. In an era defined by uncertainty and constant comparison, this book is a balm, reminding readers that renewal is possible, that their story is not over, and that beginnings can emerge from the very places we try hardest to forget.

Becoming Again is more than a memoir. It is a companion for anyone seeking courage, clarity, and a fresh start. I am confident it will inspire countless young people to rewrite their narrative with honesty, faith, and hope.

Idris Ayodeji Bello

Afropreneur & Founding Partner, LoftyInc Capital

Becoming Again is a powerful and poignant memoir that chronicles Abdulbasit Abdusalam's journey of self-discovery, resilience, and redemption. The author's honest and vulnerable writing style makes his story relatable and easy to connect with on a deep level.

Abdulbasit's ability to distill complex emotions into simple insights is a unique aspect of the book. He shares valuable lessons on perseverance, self-forgiveness, and trusting one's potential, adding depth and nuance to the narrative. The book is divided into four parts: Falling, Failing, Finding, and Becoming, each exploring a stage of renewal and growth.

The author's willingness to confront his vulnerabilities and imperfections is inspiring. He portrays failure and struggle unflinchingly, yet is unapologetic about his successes and growth. This authenticity makes the book feel like a conversation with a friend who has been through the wringer and come out stronger.

Overall, Becoming Again is a beautifully written, thought-provoking, and uplifting book that will resonate with anyone facing setbacks, self-doubt, or uncertainty. Abdulbasit's story is a testament to the human spirit's capacity for resilience, growth, and transformation. I highly recommend it to anyone seeking inspiration, guidance, or a reminder that they are not alone in their struggles.

Engineer Idris Lawal Akinremi
Director of Structures, Advanced Engineering Consultants.

In a world obsessed with polished success stories on social media, the struggles behind those triumphs are rarely seen. How can we understand someone's journey or measure our own when failure is hidden and only victory is celebrated? Abdulbasit Abdusalam offers a fresh and fearless perspective. He reveals the power of failure, the lessons hidden in setbacks, and the strength that comes from "becoming again." Failure is not the end. It is the spark to fight back, the chance to rewrite your story, take bold steps forward, and transform mistakes into momentum.

In Becoming Again, Abdulbasit deconstructs the myth of starting from zero. He shows that every failure is a foundation built on experience and reminds us that experience is the greatest teacher. The wheel of success is in our hands, and the future is not something to wait for but something we create.

Ibrahim Nureni
Cofounder, Mind Thrive Africa

Dedication

To Allah, the One who found me in my lowest place, and with whose mercy anything broken can be rebuilt.

And to everyone who stood beside me when life bent me out of shape: my family, my lovely wife, my mentors, and my friends. Your belief kept my story alive long enough for me to become again.

Foreword I

Holding this book in your hands is like holding a testimony that was earned, not imagined. It carries the weight of a man I have known for most of his life. I remember Abdulbasit long before life introduced him to its harsh turns. He was a boy with a restless curiosity, the kind that made you sure he would grow into every possibility laid before him. His journey looked like it would be a straight line of progress, moving steadily from promise to fulfilment.

I watched him begin his university education with the confidence that comes from sincere effort. He walked in carrying the hopes of his family and the calm belief that his future was secure. Then the line bent. The day the news reached him that he had been advised to withdraw, it did not land like an academic setback. It landed like an earthquake. It was the kind of moment where everything goes blank, a distasteful experience that nobody wants to associate with, and you are left alone with the uncomfortable space between who you thought you were and what life has just revealed.

But what followed was not the fall people expected. Instead of running from the shame, the disappointment, and the questions, he faced them. He was happy to accept his fault in all of the failures and ready to redeem himself. That season of dropping out, confronting his weaknesses, and later gathering the courage to start again in a different institution, was when he started reconstructing himself. It was the slow, sometimes painful work of taking out what was broken and rebuilding from a place of honesty.

By the time he completed that journey, he was no longer the same person who began years before. He was wiser, committed, and more compassionate. The failure, the pain, and the faith that carried him through shaped a depth in him that is evident in every chapter of this book.

This is a book about coming home to yourself after losing your way. Becoming Again captures the ache of regret, the beauty of surrender, and the sacred work of rebuilding a life with intention. It is a companion for anyone longing to rediscover their worth.

It comes from someone who has been to the low places, who has questioned his worth, who has felt lost, and who has wondered if repair was still possible. There are no shortcuts or shiny solutions in this book. What you will find instead is a patient roadmap for the inner work that transforms a life. It is a reminder that failure is not a dead end. It is a difficult teacher, but a necessary one.

If you are reading this while feeling stuck or ashamed or convinced that your window of possibility has closed, this book is a gentle but firm intervention. It is a reminder that being able to begin again is one of God's most generous gifts. It teaches that sometimes the only way to find the life meant for you is to let your first idea of success crumble.

May this book give you the courage to be truthful with yourself, the strength to release what no longer serves you, and the patience to grow into the person you are becoming.
A long-time friend who has seen the journey from the beginning,

Dr Sulaimon Ogunmuyiwa
Chairman, Board of Incorporated Trustees, First Class Muslim Foundation

Foreword II

On a bright afternoon in 2019, Abdulbasit told me he had been asked to withdraw from the Geoscience department at the University of Lagos. What struck me that day wasn't the setback itself, but the clarity of his response to it. Without hesitation, he said, "I'll start preparing for the next JAMB. I'm choosing Lagos State University and Economics." There was no self-pity, no pause. He already had a plan to rise again. He didn't even give me the chance to feel bad on his behalf; instead, he handed me a roadmap of what came next.

A few months ago, one of my closest childhood friends reached out, overwhelmed by the desire to "become again." Not long after, Abdulbasit committed his own journey and lessons into this book – a guide that, in many ways, became the answer my friend was searching for.

Many people struggle with restarting their lives because of the fear of the unknown. Yet they forget that the same uncertainty exists for those who continue moving without direction, clarity, or purpose. Starting again is not a sign of failure – it is an act of courage.

One of the many things that resonates with me in this book is its honest acknowledgement of failures. The book is not here to give us a sugar-coated version of life – how you seamlessly graduate from secondary school, gain admission into the university, land a six-figure job with a top multinational, and marry the best woman in the world. No, it's not about that. There is a clear acknowledgement of failure, of guilt, and of shame, yet an understanding that moving on quickly and choosing to become again is one of the best decisions you can make as a human being.

This reminds me of one of my favourite verses of the Qur'an in Suratul Az-Zumar, where Allah says, "Say: O My servants who have transgressed against themselves, do not despair of the mercy of Allah. Indeed, Allah forgives all sins. Indeed, it is He who is the Forgiving, the Merciful." This emphasises that it is normal to fail but allowing yourself to be consumed by it is wrong.

Becoming Again is a powerful and necessary book. I would recommend it not only to those who feel lost or stuck, but also to those who believe they are on the right path. The lessons within these pages hold the potential to strengthen future decisions, inspire renewed purpose, and remind us that beginning again is always possible.

Hassan Salaudeen
Tech Consultant, KPMG

Introduction

There are seasons in life when everything you once believed about yourself begins to shift. The plans that once made perfect sense suddenly lose their meaning, and the confidence you carried gradually fades. You question the choices you made, the path you took, and even the faith that once grounded you. For most people, this season arrives without warning. It does not always come through a tragedy or public collapse. Sometimes, it begins in the silence of your thoughts the slow realisation that you have lost direction.

I have lived through such a season. It began during a time when I thought I had everything under control. I had just started university, full of the optimism and certainty that comes with youth. My path looked clear, my goals defined, and my ambition sincere. I believed that if I worked hard enough and stayed consistent, everything would fall into place. But life does not always unfold in straight lines; sometimes an unexpected detour changes everything you thought you knew about yourself.

When I received the message that I had failed and was advised to withdraw, I had no idea how to respond. It didn't seem real at first. I remember reading it over and over again, waiting for a different outcome. It never came. In that moment, I realised that failure has a way of revealing who you really are when the applause stops and the plans fall apart. I had always imagined that failure was something that happened to careless people or those who did not try hard enough. I never thought it could happen to me, not because I was perfect, but because I believed effort alone was enough. It was that experience that taught me that effort without focus is noise and that passion without discipline is only potential.

What followed was one of the quietest periods of my life. I did not want to talk about it. I avoided questions and withdrew from people who used to look up to me. The shame was heavy, not just because of what I had lost, but because of what I thought it said about me. In a world that celebrates achievement, failure feels like exile. No one prepares you for how isolating it can be to feel like you no longer belong in the spaces that once defined you.

During that period, I came face-to-face with my limitations. I began to understand how easy it is to build your identity around success. When everything is going well, it is easy to believe that you are strong and capable. But when life pauses when you have nothing to prove or perform you are forced to ask harder questions: Who am I without achievements? What do I truly value when the world stops clapping? Those questions became the foundation of a deeper transformation I did not see coming.

This book reflects that transformation. It was not written to glorify pain or to romanticise failure, but to show that they can be teachers. I believe that everyone, at some point, will face a version of that defining pause a moment where life forces you to confront the distance between who you are and who you thought you would be. For some, it comes through career disappointment. For others, it comes through heartbreak, burnout, spiritual dryness, or the awakening realisation that their life is moving forward but not fulfilling.

We live in a time when it is easier to appear fine than to be actually fine. Social media has taught us how to curate the image of progress, even when we are internally exhausted. Many people are silently battling feelings of inadequacy and confusion while pretending to have it all together. The result is a generation of people who are outwardly successful but inwardly lost. I know this because I have been there. I know what it means to smile publicly while privately feeling like I have lost the thread of my story.

Becoming Again was written for that space between external success and internal struggle. It is for those who are tired of pretending, for those who feel spiritually disconnected, and for those who want to start again but do not know how. This is not a book about quick recovery. It is about the slow, often uncomfortable process of rebuilding your life from the inside out. It is about rediscovering meaning after loss and understanding that growth is not always visible. Sometimes, the real transformation happens low-key, away from people's applause, in the stillness of your reflection.

When I look back on my journey now, I see that failure was not my enemy. It was a mirror that revealed parts of me I would never have noticed otherwise. It showed me the danger of living for approval and the emptiness of progress without peace. Most importantly, it taught me the difference between working hard and working wisely. I began to understand that the true measure of success is not how high you climb, but how deeply you are rooted when things fall apart.

Faith became an anchor during that process, though not in the dramatic way people often describe it. There was no sudden revelation or voice from the heavens. Instead, faith returned slowly through reflection, prayer, and the realisation that God's mercy is not limited to our performance. I learnt that God is not only present in victory.

He is equally near in confusion, in delay, and in disappointment. The Qur'an says, "Do not despair of the mercy of Allah. Indeed, Allah forgives all sins." That verse became a comfort to me, not only in a religious sense but also in a personal one. It reminded me that grace is not something we earn; it is something we receive.

Many people believe that once they have failed, they have lost the right to dream again. They feel unworthy of a second chance because they assume God's patience has limits. However, I have come to believe that the opportunity to begin again is one of life's greatest gifts. Starting over does not erase the past; it redeems it. The mistakes do not disappear, but they stop defining you. They become part of your testimony, not your identity.

This book is an attempt to share what that process looks like. Each chapter explores a stage of renewal, what it feels like to lose, reflect, rediscover, and finally, rebuild. You will find stories from my life, moments of clarity drawn from experience, and reflections on faith that guided me through those seasons. As you read, I hope that you will find pieces of yourself in these pages.

I wrote this book because I know what it means to lose your way. I know how it feels to question your worth, to doubt your purpose, and to wonder if you have disappointed God beyond repair. I also know what it means to stand up again not with pride, but with peace. I learnt that growth begins with honesty, and that honesty sometimes looks like admitting that you do not have all the answers.

As you begin this journey, read slowly. Reflect as you go. Some parts of this book may challenge you, others may comfort you, but all are written with the hope that you see your story differently. You do not need to have everything figured out to move forward. You only need the willingness to start.

We often underestimate the subtle power of small beginnings. It is easy to overlook the progress that happens within. But every time you choose to forgive yourself, to pray again, or to take one more step after falling, you are becoming again.

If there is one truth that runs through this entire book, it is this: you are not beyond redemption. Life has a way of circling back to the things we thought we lost. Grace has a way of reaching the places we thought were too damaged to be touched. Your story may have paused, but it has not ended. There is still room for you to rebuild, to rediscover, and to return.

Becoming Again is about possibilities. It is the assurance that no matter how far you have fallen, you can rise again as someone wiser, calmer, and more grounded in faith.

So, as you turn the page, I want you to take a deep breath and release the weight of what has been. You do not have to rush this process. Healing takes time. Becoming takes patience. But if you stay open, you will find that what you once called failure was only the beginning of something greater.

This is where that journey begins.

Author's Note: To the Reader Who Feels Lost

If you are holding this book and reading these words, there is a chance that something in your life feels uncertain. Perhaps you are at a crossroads, or maybe you are standing in the middle of something that no longer feels familiar. It might be the loss of direction, a mistake that keeps echoing in your mind, or the lingering fatigue that comes from trying to be strong for too long. Whatever it is, I want you to know that you are not alone.

When I began writing this book, I was not trying to sound wise. I was trying to make sense of my silence. I had lived through moments when life did not go as planned, and I no longer knew where to turn. The pages that follow were written from that place not from certainty, but from sincerity. I wanted to capture what it truly feels like to fall, to fail, and to rebuild.

This book will not give you formulas. It will not tell you that everything will change overnight. But it will remind you that change is still possible. It will show you that renewal is rarely sudden; it is a gradual process of becoming honest with yourself again. It begins the moment you stop pretending that everything is fine and start listening to what your soul is trying to say.

If you feel lost, I hope these words become a steady companion. You do not have to rush to understand everything. You do not have to fix yourself immediately. You only need to take the next small step, no matter how uncertain it feels. Healing is not a single event; it is a slow unfolding.

As you read, I hope you pause when something resonates. Write your reflections, cry if you must, and pray if you can.

Allow yourself to feel. The path to peace is never about forgetting what happened but remembering the person you are becoming because of it.

You have not gone too far. You have not failed too deeply. Your story is not over yet.

You can still become again.

—— Chapter One: ——
When the Light Went Out

"So verily, with hardship comes ease."
Qur'an 94:5

It began on an ordinary Tuesday evening. I had finished praying and was sitting near the rear of the mosque to gather my thoughts before heading to the hostel. A classmate came by, looked around, and walked towards me with the careful steps of someone carrying difficult news. He leaned slightly and spoke low enough for only me to hear. Our results had been reviewed. The department had made its decision. I had been advised to withdraw.

For a moment, I couldn't arrange the words into meaning. I asked him to repeat himself. He did, with the same hushed tone. There was no accusation in his eyes, only the uncomfortable sympathy people wear when they are forced to deliver what they did not cause. I looked lost as he left. I stood up and walked out without looking back. The walkway outside the mosque felt longer than usual. A group of students laughed near the entrance. Someone argued on the phone. A lecturer's car rolled past with the radio turned up. The world continued as if the ground had not shifted beneath my feet.

I returned to the hostel and lay on my bed. The fan turned slowly above me. My mind began to play back small choices that now felt consequential—the nights I spent scrolling mindlessly, the lectures I missed because I believed I could catch up later, and the times I did the minimum because there would always be another week to come correct. It's easy to say "later" when life still looks wide; it becomes difficult when the margins close.

That night, sleep did not come. I rehearsed explanations to my mentors and then erased them. I imagined the looks on my friends' faces. I tried to find an angle that would make the story sound less like a failure and more like an "unfortunate" event. Nothing sounded honest. At some point, I stopped trying and stared at the ceiling in silence. I understood that some moments do not need commentary. They ask for recognition and then responsibility.

Morning arrived, and I did what many people do when life unravels: I chose to look composed. I showered, dressed neatly, and stepped out with a calm face. I answered messages. I said, "I am fine," to people who asked how I was doing, because the question was routine and the answer was easier than explaining the truth. That week turned into several weeks. The smile continued. The habits continued. The pretence became a shield. At night, the shield dissolved and the weight returned. During the day, I carried out responsibilities as if the centre had not shifted.

The hardest part was the slow redefinition of self that follows public disappointment. You begin to wonder if the person people thought you were ever existed, or if you were an image held together by early success and expectations. You feel the pressure of narratives, family hopes, and your ambition. You see how quickly people move on, and fair enough, because everyone is carrying something of their own. The crowd does not linger long around anyone's private storm.

It is common to associate failure with noise, smashing plates, and raised voices. Mine arrived quietly. It walked into the room and sat beside me as if it had always had a chair there. In that quiet, I remembered a verse I had known since childhood but had never needed as I did then. The Qur'an says, "Indeed, man was created in hardship." The verse is neither a threat nor an excuse. It is a description of reality. Life is not designed to be without weight. The admission of that fact did not remove the sting, but it removed the surprise. Pain hurts more when you believe it has no right to be there.

There is a particular kind of shame that takes root in societies that prioritise outcomes over process. We often portray success without context, leading people who are having trouble to believe that their struggles are a character flaw. Comparison sharpens it. On social media, it appears that everyone is moving forward quickly. People highlight their wins: high grades, new roles, and curated moments of joy. It is natural to be happy for them. Also, when your life seems to be stagnant, it's normal to question where you went wrong. In that season, I discovered that shame weighs more than failure. Failure is a result. Shame is a story you tell about yourself.

Before that Tuesday, I believed that effort would correct everything. I trusted my ability to do well when I needed to. I assumed late sprints could fix early drift. The experience taught me that potential is not a plan and that talent is not a timetable. If you do not build structure around your goals, immediate impulses will always compete and often win. It also taught me that control is smaller than it feels. I could make choices, but I could not choose their consequences. I could prepare, but I could not own the outcomes. The Qur'an contains a piece of counsel that initially struck me as harsh, yet unfolded as mercy with time. "Perhaps you dislike something which is good for you, and perhaps you love something which is bad for you. Allah knows while you do not know." Time reframed those words for me. I did not have to call a setback good to accept that it could become useful. In the first few weeks, I said little to anyone. When I finally sat before one of my mentors, he did not humiliate me. He spoke to me about failure and the importance of getting back up after failure. I left his place relieved. However, I still had to face the reality that there was a detour in my journey. I still had to watch my peers proceed without me.

There is a kind of loneliness that does not require distance from people. You can be in a room full of friends and still feel it. It arrives when you realise that a decision has been made about your life, and you are the one who must answer for it. In that loneliness, I began to notice details I usually missed. The silent walk from the hostel to the faculty building. The dull sound of ceiling fans in empty classrooms. The way the campus emptied in the late afternoon and grew alive again in the evening. I watched the world and saw what pain does to perception. It makes ordinary things clearer. It forces you to pay attention.

I began to read again. Not course notes. Books about discipline, focus, and the ordinary effort that produces steady progress. I returned to the Qur'an with a different posture, not to find verses that predicted my rescue, but to learn the kind of person I should become so that rescue would not be wasted. I made two small practices non-negotiable. I prayed with focus, even when it felt dry. I journalled without performance, writing sentences that were sometimes ugly but honest.

People often ask what to do first after a failure that bends one's path. I do not have a universal answer. I can only say what helped me. I listed the habits that had weakened my direction. I reduced the hours I spent online. I limited the number of events I attended. I learnt to schedule study before social commitments, not after them. It sounds technical because it was technical. Grand declarations rarely change a life. Simple rules applied consistently do.

Starting again requires a decision that sounds simple but is not easy. You need to agree that the old version of your life has ended and that you will not waste your energy trying to resurrect it. In my case, I had to accept that I would sit in classrooms with people younger than I am, that I would be reminded of lost time, and that I would see former classmates move ahead while I return to the beginning. If you waste energy resenting this, you will not have the energy to rebuild. Humility is a skill as much as a virtue. It allows you to learn without the noise of image management.

I used to hear the claim that "starting over" meant "starting from scratch". That is not accurate. You never start from zero after a fall if you are willing to extract the lessons. You start from experience. You have seen what happens when you drift. You have felt the cost of delay. You have learnt where your day disappears when it is not protected. That knowledge is not a small thing. If you use it, your second beginning can be stronger than your first.

It is helpful to avoid romanticising failure. There is nothing noble in missing your responsibilities when they could have been avoided. Nothing is inspiring about repeating the same patterns and calling it perseverance. There is a difference between a fall that becomes an education and a fall that becomes a cycle. The first requires honesty, structure, and accountability. The second resists all three.

The Qur'an says, "O you who believe, seek help through patience and prayer. Indeed, Allah is with the patient." Patience is not passive waiting. In the most practical sense, it is controlled consistency. It is showing up and doing what you said you would do when emotions are low and applause is absent. Prayer at such times is alignment. You ask for strength to carry the weight that is yours to bear and clarity to let go of what is not.

I realised one morning in my second year of starting over that I had stopped acting fine because I felt fine. It did not arrive with fanfare. I was reviewing notes and suddenly noticed that a calm steadiness had replaced earlier panic. Confidence, the useful kind, is often this quiet. It does not need a display because it is built on practice rather than performance.

Looking back at the earlier withdrawal, I do not call it good. I call it instructive. There is a difference. Pain is not good, but it can be fruitful if you respond with responsibility. The experience cured me of certain illusions. It cured me of the idea that I could run on raw ability. It cured me of the desire to appear busy. It cured me of the urge to chase every invitation. It taught me the cost of saying yes without criteria. It also taught me that God's mercy does not always feel like a gift when it arrives. Sometimes, mercy takes the form of removal. Sometimes, love closes a door you refuse to stop pushing.

The verse that echoed most in that period came from Surah Ash-Sharh. "For indeed, with hardship there is ease. Indeed, with hardship there is ease." The repetition is not accidental. Ease accompanies; it does not merely follow. Initially, I sought ease in the form of new circumstances. Later, I learnt to recognise ease in the form of new understanding and new strength. The pressure did not disappear; my capacity simply grew around it.

When I finally graduated, I realised the certificate mattered but the person I had become mattered more. The simple rules I adopted saved me from my worst habits. My second attempt at university did not erase my earlier experience. Instead, it reframed it. I could finally say that the earlier failure was part of my education not just a theoretical one, but a personal education, the kind that builds a life.

There is a social expectation to present success as if it were always intentional. It is better to admit that you were redirected. It is better to admit you needed correction. It is better to admit that beginning again gave you a second chance at character, not only at credentials. When we tell the truth about our rebuilding, we permit others to start their own.

If you are in the middle of a difficult chapter, you do not need a dramatic master plan to move forward; instead, you just need one clear decision, one small practice, and some time. Everyone I admire has experienced loss, confusion, or interruption. The difference between those who grow and those who repeat is not talent but honesty, patience, and the willingness to make simple changes and protect them.

A short word on disappointment and faith. Nowadays, it's common to gauge faith based on emotional certainty. When emotions collapse, people assume faith has collapsed. My experience was different. Emotions did collapse. Faith continued as an act of obedience when feelings were grey. The prayers were not loud. The verses were not easy. Yet the practice continued. Over time, emotion returned, this time more stable because it was not the driver. If you wait to feel inspired before doing what is right, you will often abandon the right thing to do. However, if you do what is right because it is right, inspiration usually returns with respect.

There is a hadith that defines strength in a way that helped me reset my idea of success. The Prophet Muhammad, peace be upon him, said that the strong person is not the one who overpowers others but the one who controls himself when angry. Anger includes more than rage. It includes ego when embarrassed, panic when plans fail, and the inner aggression that lashes out when life says no. Strength in this definition is intimate. It is the ability to hold your posture when your environment changes. By that measure, the months following my withdrawal were the most empowering of my life since they demanded self-control, not applause.

At this point, it may be useful to make several observations that cost me much to learn. First, the past is not a prophecy. It's a record. Depending on how you interpret them, records have the power to either enlighten or enslave you. The second is that when you accept responsibility early on, people forgive you more quickly. Repair is delayed by defensiveness. The third is that simple systems outperform inspiration over time. The fourth is that being grateful is a tactic rather than a sentiment. When you can identify what is left in your hands, you will always perform better.

Some people insist that you should not talk about failure while you are still close to it. There is wisdom in letting distance shape your words, but there is also value in telling the truth while memory is fresh. Memory that is too distant can become edited by pride. A recent memory can be sharpened by humility. I am telling this as it happened so that the reader, who may be inside their ordinary Tuesday, can see that this is not the end of the path it is a bend.

When I think about that classmate who delivered the news, I feel grateful to him. Someone had to tell me. Someone had to be the voice that shifted the story forward. It has stayed with me as a principle. Deliver truth gently and accept truth with courage. A life that avoids unpleasant facts will soon be ruled by them. A life that learns to face them can change them.

The decision to begin again was not noble. It was necessary. I registered. I studied. I protected the mornings and reduced the evening noise. I learnt to leave places earlier than I wanted to because there was work to do. I wrote small reviews at the end of the week. What did I do well? Where did I drift? What will I change on Monday? These questions became anchors against self-deception. Growth is not only about trying harder. It is also about measuring honestly.

It is tempting to conclude a chapter like this with a sweeping sentence that promises ease if you do what I did. I will not do that. I am not the measure, and life is not symmetrical. Your story will have different constraints and different timing. What I can say is simple and sincere. You are not disqualified by a fall. If you treat it as a teacher instead of a label, it will produce fruit. If you respond with consistency instead of dramatic vows, you will see change. If you ask God for help

and then act in line with that prayer, you will become someone you respect. Becoming is the real goal. Certificates, titles, and comments follow as they choose.
There is a final verse that belongs here, not as decoration, but as a promise that has rescued many. "Say, O My servants who have transgressed against themselves, do not despair of the mercy of Allah. Indeed, Allah forgives all sins." The verse addresses the person who knows they are responsible for the mess they are in. It does not minimise the wrong. It widens the door. You can walk through it. The act of walking is not poetic. It is practical. It looks like deleting a distraction. It looks like choosing one difficult task before noon. It looks like praying even when your throat is dry. It looks like sending a message to a mentor and accepting feedback without defence. It looks like telling the truth about your day to yourself.

If there is one picture I keep from that first evening, it is the short walk from the mosque to the open air outside. The air was the same. The walkway was the same. I was not. I had heard news that required a decision about the kind of person I would be. The decision took months to mature, but it began there. If you are reading this while standing at your threshold, let me say what I wish someone had said to me: do not rush, but do not delay. Sit with the truth. Ask God for help. Make one honest plan. Begin again.

The light went out that night. It returned differently. It did not return as brightness alone. It returned as clarity. It returned as the ability to say no without guilt. It returned as careful choices that freed hours. It returned as a concentration I did not know I could cultivate. It returned as faith that no longer depended on public moments. It returned as a new respect for ordinary days.

If the purpose of this chapter is to answer one question, it is this. Can a life recover after a public fall? The answer is yes, if recovery is defined not by erasing the past but by learning from it, and not by impressing others but by building habits that make relapse unlikely. Recovery is neither quick nor linear. It remains possible, and in many cases, it produces a deeper person than an uninterrupted success story would have done.

I am closing this chapter not with victory, but with direction. Chapter Two explores the silence that follows the first shock. Silence is not empty. It is instructive for you to learn how to sit in it without panic. Before we go there, take a minute to face your life with the seriousness it deserves and the mercy it requires.

Reflection Section

- Think about a time something important to you ended suddenly. What did that moment reveal about your expectations and your dependence on control?
- How often do you pretend to be fine when you are not? What might change if you allowed yourself to be honest—first with yourself, then with God?
- What does patience mean to you? Is it waiting for things to improve or trusting that God's wisdom is already at work?
- Remember: Light does not disappear; it only changes form. Sometimes, it returns as understanding. Sometimes, it returns as peace.

Chapter Two:
The Silence After the Storm

"Let silence take you to the core of life."
Rumi

Silence often arrives uninvited. It does not knock or introduce itself. It simply enters after the noise of crisis fades, when everyone who came to comfort you has gone home, and the conversations about your situation have run their course. What follows is not peace, at least not at first. It is a strange emptiness. The messages slow down, the questions stop coming, and suddenly, the world seems to forget that your life just changed.

That silence feels heavy. It does not feel like stillness; it feels like absence. It was in that space, after the news had settled, that I began to live inside my thoughts for the first time.

For a while, I misunderstood what was happening. I thought silence meant that failure had finished its work and nothing else was left to learn. But silence is not the end of the story; it is the classroom where the next lesson begins.

After any fall, there is a brief season of attention. People reach out, ask how you are doing, and offer advice or sympathy. Then, slowly, their lives call them back. You can't blame them for it. Everyone is fighting their personal battles. But the shift is difficult to accept. You go from being surrounded by people to realising that the burden you bear is now solely your own.

That was the hardest part not the event itself, but the days after, when life became unbearably normal. The sun still rose, classes were still held, and even markets still opened. Life did not pause to match my mood.

I used to walk around campus in those days, observing how easily the world continued. That experience taught me something uncomfortable but necessary: that pain does not make you special. It makes you human. The world's indifference is not cruelty; it is simply the nature of life. Things keep moving. People keep going.

That realisation was sobering, but it carried mercy. It reminded me that healing would not depend on the attention of others. It would depend on what I did with the silence that remained.

Before that season, I was not comfortable with silence. I always needed something going on or endless scrolling through my phone. I equated this with normalcy. If my phone was not buzzing, I felt left out. I felt idle when I wasn't conversing with anyone.

It is a common condition of our generation. We are constantly plugged in, checking notifications, switching between screens, and scrolling without purpose. Silence feels strange because it exposes what we have been avoiding. When the noise stops, we begin to hear ourselves, and not everyone likes what they hear.

After the withdrawal, I could not distract myself the same way anymore. The usual escapes no longer numbed me. They made the noise louder. The moment I put my phone down, my thoughts returned sharper than before.

That is when I realised how much I had depended on noise to avoid reflection. Most of us are not afraid of silence itself; we are afraid of what it will reveal about us.

Silence shows you the gap between what you say and what you do. It exposes the compromises you've made, the promises you never kept, and the feelings you've buried under productivity. It does not flatter you. It confronts you.
But if you stay long enough, silence also starts to heal you. It teaches you to listen differently not for replies, but for understanding.

Learning the Difference Between Loneliness and Solitude
In the beginning, I mistook silence for loneliness. The days felt long, and the absence of constant chatter made the world feel distant. But over time, I began to see that loneliness and solitude are not the same thing. Loneliness is emptiness; solitude is awareness.

Loneliness asks, Who will be with me? Solitude asks, Who am I becoming when I am alone?

There is a verse in the Qur'an that says, "And in yourselves, do you not see?" It is an invitation to pay attention to the world around you and the inner workings of your life. Solitude gives you that chance.

It was in solitude that I began to rebuild small habits of thought. I wrote more. I read intentionally. I began to pray without rushing because I needed somewhere to place the weight. I started taking evening walks to think clearly.

During one of those walks, I realised how much noise I had used to avoid responsibility. The constant activity, the over commitment, the endless online presence all of it had kept me from asking the real questions.

Who was I outside achievement? What did I truly want? What kind of person was I becoming?

Silence creates accountability. It becomes difficult to lie to yourself when you can finally hear your voice clearly.

When Silence Feels Like Punishment

There is a stage after failure that no one prepares you for. It is not the guilt. It is not the public embarrassment. It's the empty gap that follows the feeling that nothing is happening.

Days pass, and you can't point to progress. You start to wonder whether God has gone silent, too. You pray, but the answers do not arrive in the form you expect. You try to concentrate, but your mind drifts back to the past. You begin to think the silence is punishment.

When everything goes mute, it may mean that life is giving you space to recover before the next chapter begins. It is the pause between the injury and the healing, the stillness before a new direction.

In retrospect, I see that I would have quickly returned to my old habits if things had improved right away following that fall. The silence slowed me down long enough to learn. It forced me to live without shortcuts.

Our generation often sees silence as failure. We call it stagnation; we measure progress by activity. Sometimes, stillness is the only environment where growth can begin.

The Modern Escape

It is difficult to talk about silence today without confronting our addiction to distraction. We are the most connected generation in history, and yet, arguably, the least at peace.
The average person cannot sit in a room for ten minutes without reaching for a screen. We check our phones not out of curiosity but out of habit. We open social media, scroll

through other people's highlights, and in the process, silence becomes unbearable.

Distraction has become our modern comfort zone. We use it to avoid thinking about who we have become. We use it to escape boredom, but boredom is often the first sign that our minds are trying to rest.

In that season of my life, I began to detox from noise gradually. I turned off notifications. I deleted a few apps temporarily. I stopped listening to background noise while studying. It was awkward at first, like learning to breathe again. But slowly, I noticed that my thoughts began to stretch again. I could focus longer. I remembered more. I started to notice patterns in my thinking, the ones that pushed me toward anxiety and the ones that led me toward calm.

Modern silence must be chosen. It doesn't arrive naturally anymore. We have to fight for it.

The discipline of being quiet is resistance against the culture of constant stimulation that makes it difficult to think deeply or feel honestly.

Listening to Life Again

After the first few weeks of silence, I began to notice things I had missed before. The sound of birds at dawn. The faint hum of power lines in the evening. The rhythm of my breathing.

It may sound simple, but this awareness matters. The small details of life remind you that the world is still full of movement, even when your plans are not.

Silence also helped me pay attention to other people

differently. I listened more. I stopped rushing to respond in conversations. I learnt that listening is a form of respect for others and for yourself. It trains you to wait before reacting.

There was wisdom in the way the Prophet Muhammad, peace be upon him, often paused before speaking. He allowed silence to clarify thought. That is something we have lost today. We speak before we think, post before we process, and argue before we understand.

In silence, I learnt restraint. I learnt that not every thought needs to be said, and not every feeling needs an audience. Some things are meant to mature in private before they are shared.

The Shape of Growth

Growth does not always begin with motivation. Sometimes, it begins with stillness, when you have nothing to prove and nowhere to go. That is where humility finds space to grow.

In those months of deep reflection, I began to see patterns in myself more clearly. I saw how impatience had guided most of my earlier decisions. I wanted everything fast: results, recognition, and validation. I mistook speed for progress. But silence slowed me down, and in that stillness, I began to notice the value of steady effort.

In Stillness Is the Key by Ryan Holiday, he mentioned, *"Stillness allows us to see clearly what's happening and respond appropriately, rather than being driven by emotion or impulse."*

I started rebuilding my life through small, consistent actions. Reading a few pages a day. Writing thoughts before sleeping. Waking up earlier to pray. These habits felt insignificant at first, but they held weight. They built rhythm.

They taught me that discipline is more reliable than motivation.

People often think healing happens suddenly, like turning on a light. In truth, it happens gradually, like dawn. You do not always notice it as it happens, but one day you realise the darkness has lifted a little.

Clarity in the Quiet

I sat outside alone one evening, months after everything had changed, and realised I was no longer bitter. I wasn't trying to explain myself. I wasn't rehearsing what-ifs. I was simply sitting, watching people pass by, feeling the breeze, and hearing laughter in the distance. For the first time, I felt at peace with not having all the answers.

That moment taught me that clarity doesn't always mean understanding why something happened. Sometimes, clarity means being able to live with what happened and still be whole.

The more I grew comfortable with silence, the more I realised that I had misjudged it. Silence was not absence; it was presence, just not the kind I was used to. It was the space where I could sense that life was still moving, even when I wasn't.

And perhaps that is what faith becomes in difficult times: the conviction that even when you can't see progress, something within you is still being formed.

Relearning How to Begin

When I eventually began to take practical steps forward, they did not feel dramatic. There was no grand comeback moment. I simply started showing up differently.

Silence had taught me patience. I no longer rushed

decisions. I evaluated opportunities before saying yes. I stopped comparing my progress to others. I began to treat effort as worship, not as performance.

When you emerge from silence, you begin to understand that doing less can mean achieving more. You begin to choose depth over appearance. You realise that not every season is for action; some are for listening, some for learning, and some simply for being.

The silence after my storm did not erase the pain of what happened, but it changed my relationship with pain. It taught me to stop viewing every setback as an emergency. Some setbacks are actually invitations to slow down and see differently.

The Discipline of Quiet Progress

Our culture rewards visibility. If it is not posted, it is assumed not to exist. But real transformation often happens away from the spotlight. In the years that followed, I noticed a pattern among people who matured gracefully after disappointment. They all had a season of quiet rebuilding, a period when they withdrew, not to escape, but to grow without distraction.

The silence after the storm is where integrity forms. It is where you decide whether your next chapter will be built on resentment or wisdom. It is where you learn that validation is fragile and that peace is the only lasting success. You cannot bypass silence and still expect depth.

The writer Rumi once said, "The quieter you become, the more you can hear." I believe that. But I would add that the quieter you become, the more you can become—because stillness creates room for identity to settle, clarity to grow, and faith to take root again.

Years later, when I think about that quiet season, I do not see emptiness anymore. I see training. I see the development of patience, gratitude, and discernment. Silence taught me that peace is not the absence of problems; it is the ability to stay grounded while they exist. It taught me that success built on noise will collapse under silence, but success built on stillness will survive chaos. It taught me that you do not need the world to understand your journey for it to be valid. Some chapters will only make sense in hindsight, and that's fine.

Above all, it taught me that you can survive silence, and not just survive it but grow through it.

Reflection Section: A Moment to Pause

- How comfortable are you with silence? What do you usually use to fill it?
- Think of a recent season where life felt slow or uneventful. What did that period reveal about your priorities?
- When was the last time you went a day without unnecessary noise? What happened inside you?
- If you could separate loneliness from solitude, what might you begin to hear more clearly?
- Are there areas of your life where you confuse movement with progress?
- What is one distraction you could reduce this week to make more space for reflection?
- In your current silence, what might be forming that you cannot yet see?

—— Chapter Three: ——
The Weight of Expectations

"I am not what happened to me. I am what I choose to become." Carl Jung

When you fall, the first thing you notice is not always the pain; it is the eyes watching you. People rarely mean harm, but their expectations become mirrors you cannot avoid. Every look, every question, and every silence carries weight. Some are heavy with disappointment, others with concern, and a few with curiosity. But they all remind you that your story is no longer just yours.

I did not tell my parents about my withdrawal until I had gotten another admission almost a year later. When I told them, I could see the disappointment on their faces, but they still tried to be positive about it and wished me well. But there were some pauses and silence.

That silence said more than any conversation could. It was not anger; it was worry. Nigerian parents rarely know how to express disappointment in words. They express it in pauses and in sighs, and suddenly they start using your local name (oríkì).

That evening, the house felt quiet. I could feel their concern in the silence that followed. They didn't ask many questions; perhaps they didn't know how to, or perhaps they understood that I was already asking myself harder ones.

In their eyes, I saw two things at once: love and expectation. They had believed in my dreams and invested their hope in my education, and now they were trying to reconcile pride with confusion. They wanted to encourage me, but they also needed time to understand what had happened.

Long after the conversation was over, I couldn't shake that silence. That night, it followed me to bed and stayed with me, reminding me that expectations are not always imposed by others. Sometimes, we build them ourselves, layer upon layer, until they become walls we can barely breathe behind. Growing up, success was described in specific, measurable ways. Graduate on time. Get a decent job. Earn well. Support your family. Do not embarrass your surname.

No one wrote these rules down, but they were clear. They guided conversations and determined who was praised and who was pitied. You didn't have to be told directly that failure was shameful; you learnt it by observing how others were spoken about.

Every culture has its version of this script. Ours simply wrapped it in love. Parents said, "I just want you to have a better life than I did." It sounded simple, even noble. But within that statement were layers of anxiety and history, years of financial struggle, societal judgement, and the need to prove that their sacrifices were not wasted.

When I fell short, I felt as though I had betrayed generations of hope. That realisation shaped how I carried myself afterwards. I became obsessed with appearing stable, competent, and "okay". I didn't want anyone's sympathy; I wanted to prove that I was fine.

But pretending to be fine is one of the heaviest expectations you can carry.

The Pressure to Prove

After failure, you begin to perform recovery. You show up

smiling, stay busy, post selectively, and drop casual updates that make you sound like you are moving forward. You tell people, "I'm figuring things out," when in truth you are still lost.

I have seen it in many others, friends who left school discreetly, who stayed off social media for a while and returned later with careful captions about "new beginnings". I knew what those words meant: the need to control the narrative before the narrative controlled you.

We live in a world where image is survival. Everyone is branding themselves, even without meaning to. Our generation has learnt to speak in curated sentences: I'm building, I'm growing, I'm grateful. But underneath, many are simply trying not to drown.

I once spoke to a friend who had failed a crucial exam for the third time. He laughed as he told the story, but his eyes betrayed him. "I just don't want people to think I am unserious," he said. That sentence stayed with me because it captures a deep truth that, sometimes, our biggest fear is not failure itself but being seen as a failure.

The performance of competence is exhausting. It demands that you keep smiling while falling apart inside. It convinces you that vulnerability is weakness, that honesty is unprofessional, and that rest is laziness. Eventually, you begin to measure your worth by how well you can maintain the illusion. That illusion is heavy.

I once knew someone who studied a course she never wanted. Her parents had chosen it because it sounded respectable. She wanted to work in design; they wanted a doctor. She tried to balance both but slowly lost herself.

When we spoke one evening, she said something that I have never forgotten: "I've become so good at being who they want that I no longer know who I am."

That sentence could have been said by many people I have met since then. I have heard it in different forms, from students who switched courses to please their families, from employees who stayed in jobs that drained them, and from people who play along with their peers because they do not want to be perceived as dull.

It is not rebellion to want a life that fits you; it is responsibility. But in a society built on collective identity, individual desire often looks selfish.

This tension between duty and self-awareness is one of the hardest battles to navigate. How do you honour the people who raised you without betraying the person you are becoming?

There is no easy answer. But reflection and honesty with yourself are often where the answer begins to form.

Between Love and Expectation

Parents rarely intend harm when they pressure their children. Their expectations often come from love, the protective kind that wants to prevent future pain. For many African parents, education is not just an opportunity; it is redemption. It is the proof that their sacrifices meant something.

I learnt this gradually. When I looked beyond my shame, I began to see my father not as a critic, but as someone who wanted safety for his child. His firmness was more out of fear than control. Fear that I would face the same struggles he had fought his whole life to escape.

Understanding this did not remove the weight, but it made it easier to carry. Love, even when it comes with pressure, deserves empathy. Parents are humans too, humans trying to secure what they never had.

Still, there comes a point where you must separate gratitude from guilt. Gratitude says, "I appreciate what you've done for me." Guilt says, "I must live only to please you." The first leads to growth; the second leads to simmering resentment.

The Cost of Comparison

Every generation faces comparison, but ours faces it publicly. Social media has turned life into a performance arena. Everyone posts their highlight reel, and we scroll through, unconsciously grading ourselves.

You see people moving abroad, starting businesses, getting engaged, and buying cars. You clap for them, as you should, but somewhere in the background, a small voice asks, When will it be my turn?

That voice grows louder when you are already battling disappointment. It tells you that you are behind, that you are wasting time, and that everyone else has figured life out.

But the truth is, timelines are illusions. Everyone's pace is different because everyone's purpose is different. You may be building internally while others are building visibly. You may be growing roots while others are growing branches. Both are progress, just not the same kind.

I learnt to respect my season by limiting what I consumed. I muted accounts that made me feel inadequate. I replaced comparison with curiosity, asking myself what I could learn from people instead of envying them. I stopped competing

for pace and started competing for peace.
Comparison also blinds you to gratitude. It makes you forget how far you have come because you are too focused on how far others seem to be. You start dismissing your small victories the exam you passed, the habit you changed, the prayer you kept showing up for because they do not look dramatic enough to be celebrated. But those are the proofs that you are growing, and if you do not learn to see them, you will live in constant dissatisfaction, no matter what you achieve.

Over time, I noticed something else: the people I envied also had private burdens. Some were struggling silently with depression. Others were exhausted from chasing approval. A few admitted that their apparent "wins" were not even things they truly wanted; they just didn't want to look left behind. Everyone, in one way or another, is fighting to stay afloat. Realising this helped me see people with more compassion and myself with less judgement.

Comparison is one of the easiest ways to lose sight of God's wisdom in your life. It makes you look outward when you should be looking inward. The verse that helped me steady my mind says, "And do not wish for what Allah has given some of you over others." It reminds me that envy is as much a misunderstanding of timing as it is a lack of contentment. What is not yours now may not be meant to harm you; it may be meant to prepare you.

The day I stopped comparing, I began to breathe differently. My focus returned. My gratitude deepened. I learnt to celebrate progress without performing it, and that is how peace found me again.

When Expectation Turns Inward

Sometimes, the heaviest expectations are not external; they are the ones we place on ourselves.

I had always been the "responsible" one, the person who seemed to have it together. When I fell, I didn't just disappoint others; I disappointed my image of myself. That was harder to recover from.

We all build personal myths about who we are supposed to be. The intelligent one. The strong one. The creative one. The dependable one. When life challenges that story, the ego resists. You find yourself fighting reality because it doesn't fit the version of you that others have praised.

The process of growth, I've learnt, is also a process of unlearning. You have to release old identities that no longer serve you. You have to admit that even good qualities, like ambition, confidence, and charm, can become prisons when they are tied to performance.

There is also the hidden guilt that comes from not being who you thought you would be by a certain age. You look at your life and think, I should have grown beyond this by now. That thought can slowly drain your joy. You begin to see your life as a delay instead of a journey. But healing requires gentleness. You cannot shame yourself into transformation; you can only grow into it. The version of you that stumbled is still you, and it deserves kindness, not condemnation.

At one point, I began to track every little bit of progress I made. If I studied for two hours, I wrote it down. If I completed a task, I noted it. That record reminded me that growth is happening even when it doesn't feel dramatic. It helped me to stop treating progress as an event and start treating it as a practice.

Another lesson I learnt was that self-expectation is often rooted in comparison. I wasn't always trying to meet my standard; sometimes, I was chasing a version of success that wasn't even mine. I began to ask myself, Why do I want what I want? The answers were humbling. Some desires were genuine; others were borrowed from friends, from culture, or from the internet. Learning to tell the difference changed everything.

Eventually, I realised that forgiving myself was essential. You cannot rebuild if you keep treating your past self as an enemy. Self-forgiveness is the decision to move forward without carrying unnecessary shame. I started to speak to myself the way I would to a friend, firm but kind. That shift did not make me perfect, but it made me patient. And patience, I discovered, is the soil where real change takes root.

Redefining Success

True peace began for me the day I stopped asking, "What will people think?" and started asking, "What will I become?" Success, I realised, is not a universal measurement. It is alignment. It is when what you do matches who you are and what you believe. It is when progress no longer depends on applause.

When I entered my second degree, I decided that I would no longer live to impress anyone, not my peers, not my mentors, and not even my parents. I would live to be responsible, sincere, and disciplined. Those were standards I could control.

The funny thing is, once you stop chasing external approval, you often become more excellent. Pressure produces performance, but peace produces mastery. When your motivation shifts from fear to purpose, you begin to enjoy the work again.

I learnt that expectations will always exist. People will always have opinions. The challenge is not to escape them but to remain anchored amid them.

Redefining success also meant redefining speed. I stopped assuming that faster meant better. Some breakthroughs require long obedience; some growth can only come from seasons that feel slow. I began to measure my days by consistency, not intensity. Some days were simple: study, pray, rest, repeat. Yet those repetitive days built more progress than the chaotic ones I used to call productive.

Another shift happened when I stopped separating character from achievement. I realised that who I was becoming mattered more than what I was achieving. A good degree without discipline would still collapse under pressure. Skill without humility would eventually isolate me. But patience, gratitude, and sincerity were things that could never be taken from me. That is when success began to feel spiritual, not material.

There was also a time I thought success meant finally proving my naysayers wrong. It felt satisfying in theory but hollow in practice. Living to prove a point keeps you tied to the very voices you are trying to outgrow. You stay reactive, not creative. I learnt to shift from proving to becoming. It is never your duty to make everyone see your value; your duty is to keep growing until even silence speaks of it.

When I began to live this way, my mind grew lighter. I no longer rushed to reach milestones that didn't belong to me. I began to appreciate progress without performance. And the more I chose peace over pressure, the clearer I saw the truth: success built on serenity lasts longer than success built on stress.

Every generation inherits its own pressures. Ours is the pressure to appear successful even while learning, to always look productive even while growing, and to be constantly visible even when what we need is to be still.

But you do not owe the world a performance. You owe it the truth. You owe it effort. You owe it your best. The rest is noise. If there is one thing I want every young person to remember, it is this: expectations are not prisons unless you surrender the key. You can respect where you come from and still choose where you are going. You can love your parents without living their exact dream.

You can define your measure of success and still be faithful, grateful, and grounded.

Reflection Section: A Moment to Pause

- Whose expectations are shaping your current decisions—yours, your family's, or society's?
- What image of yourself are you still trying to protect, and what would happen if you let it go?
- When was the last time you made a choice simply because it aligned with your values, not because it looked impressive?
- Which expectations in your life are rooted in love but expressed as pressure? How can you approach them with empathy instead of anger?
- How does social media influence your sense of progress, and what boundaries could you set to regain peace?
- If you redefined success based on peace and integrity instead of pace and visibility, what would change immediately?
- Write down one expectation internal or external that you will release this week. Replace it with one intention that feels true to you.

—— Chapter Four: ——

The Disappointment Called You

"Out of suffering have emerged the strongest souls."
Khalil Gibran

There comes a moment after failure when the noise dies down and the only voice left is yours. It is not gentle. It does not ask questions. It accuses.

You replay the event in your mind a hundred times, not to understand it, but to punish yourself for it. Every version of the memory ends with the same sentence: You should have done better. You lie in bed at night, staring at the ceiling, negotiating with thoughts that refuse to rest. You remind yourself of every warning you ignored, every sign you downplayed, and every opportunity you wasted. It is a long trial with no defence.

No one needs to scold you. You have become your judge, jury, and witness.

That is what self-disappointment feels like an invisible weight that refuses to leave. It is more subtle than guilt but heavier than regret. You can be surrounded by people who say they have forgiven you, yet still feel condemned. Because shame, unlike guilt, does not attack what you did; it attacks who you are. That difference may look small, but it changes everything.

After the fall, I discovered that my greatest critic lived inside me. It wasn't the school management who had advised my withdrawal, or the classmates who whispered about it. It wasn't even my parents. It was the whispering voice in my head, the one that remembered every failure in detail and repeated it on loop.

That voice has perfect timing. It speaks just when you begin to feel normal again. It waits for moments of hope and interrupts them with reminders of who you used to be. It tells you that no matter how hard you try, you will always end up disappointing yourself again.

And the strange thing about that voice is how convincing it sounds. It doesn't yell. It whispers in logic. It reminds you of facts, timelines, and missed opportunities. It speaks the language of reason but delivers the tone of accusation.

Psychologists call this the "inner critic". I call it the echo of shame. It is the part of you that refuses to separate your actions from your identity.

The echo grows louder when you are alone, when your mind is tired, or when you see reminders of what you once dreamed of becoming. It can follow you into new seasons. You may have changed schools, jobs, or relationships, but the echo keeps asking, Who are you trying to fool? You're still the same person who failed.

Shame is not logical. It feeds on emotion and repetition. The more you listen, the more it roots itself in your mind.

The Mirror of Self-Disgust

One of the hardest things about disappointment is the way it changes how you see yourself. You begin to distrust your own reflection. Every achievement afterwards feels unearned, and every compliment sounds exaggerated. You smile, but you feel like an impostor.

That feeling is not pride; it is bruised self-trust. You start to believe that because you failed once, everything good that follows must be accidental. You live waiting for the next mistake to expose you.

This is the silent torment of many young people today. They appear confident, productive, and creative, but internally, they are battling a loss of self-belief. They doubt their intelligence, second-guess their instincts, and apologise for existing too loudly.

Shame does that. It takes away your ability to believe you can do good again. It doesn't destroy your skills; it destroys your confidence to use them.

At its worst, shame doesn't even need anyone else's opinion; you begin to carry judgement within you. You play both roles: the condemned and the condemner.

Over time, that inner disgust begins to rewrite your behaviour. You stop dreaming boldly because you do not trust your capacity to follow through. You stop setting big goals because you believe you'll ruin them. You begin to overthink simple choices, replaying worst-case scenarios that never happened. The mind becomes a courtroom where hope keeps losing the case.

It also seeps into your body. You carry yourself differently, shoulders slightly hunched, voice a little softer, presence a bit smaller. You apologise before speaking, you hesitate before trying, and you expect rejection before it arrives. The body remembers what the mind rehearses, and when you've rehearsed disappointment long enough, your posture starts to look like it.

The most dangerous part of self-disgust is how familiar it becomes. After a while, it starts to feel like honesty. You confuse low self-esteem with self-awareness. You convince yourself that being hard on yourself is the same as being responsible. But that is subtle cruelty. The mind can only bloom where it feels safe, and you cannot grow in a garden where you keep uprooting your confidence.

The Psychology of Shame

Shame thrives on identity confusion. It convinces you that you are defined by your worst moment. It fuses the temporary with the permanent. You do not say, "I failed." You say, "I am a failure."

This is why shame lingers even after circumstances improve. It responds to emotion and not evidence. You could rebuild your life, earn new accomplishments, or even gain recognition, and still feel like an impostor pretending to be redeemed.

The mind remembers humiliation more vividly than success. Neuroscientists have proven that negative experiences activate stronger emotional responses than positive ones. The brain replays embarrassment as a form of protection, hoping to prevent future pain. But the problem is that the replay never stops. You end up reliving a version of yourself that no longer exists.

Shame also distorts memory. It allows you to recall only the extremes. You forget the days you tried, the moments you improved, and the small wins that didn't make noise. Shame edits your past into a single headline: You failed.

And when that becomes your identity, it shapes how you show up in life. You start rejecting opportunities before they even arrive. You downplay your potential. You sabotage relationships because you think you'll only disappoint people again.

There is another form of shame that comes when you realise

you've become the story people use as a warning. Someone mentions your name casually as a reminder of what not to do. You overhear a reference to "people who didn't take their studies seriously", and you know they mean you.

No one has to confront you directly; the atmosphere does the work. You walk into rooms where your past has already arrived before you. You sense it in the way people avoid eye contact or lower their voices when you join a conversation.

You tell yourself it doesn't matter, but it does. You start to internalise that identity. You begin to see yourself through their eyes. You think, maybe I am the disappointment they said I was.

And once you start believing that, it becomes harder to rise again. Because shame is self-fulfilling. The more you believe you are a disappointment, the more you act like one. The more you act like one, the more others confirm it. It becomes a cycle of self-perception.

The False Comfort of Punishment

There is a strange relief that comes from self-blame. It feels like control. If everything is your fault, at least you can understand it. Punishing yourself becomes a way to make sense of the pain.

You convince yourself that you deserve the sadness, that suffering is payment for your mistake. You reject compliments. You isolate yourself from people who care. You turn down opportunities because you believe you are not ready.

In reality, self-punishment is just another disguise for fear. It allows you to avoid trying again by pretending to be moral about it. You call it humility, but it is self-sabotage.

The mind finds safety in familiar pain. You get used to disappointment because it's predictable. Hope, on the other hand, feels risky. So you cling to the familiar story of failure, not because you want to, but because it no longer surprises you.

What many people do not realise is that self-punishment can feel virtuous. It tricks you into thinking that regret is the same thing as repentance. You start to believe that feeling bad is the same as becoming better. But guilt without growth is just emotional self-harm. Pain that doesn't teach you becomes a prison.

There is also an illusion of redemption that comes with suffering. You think that if you hurt long enough, you will balance the scale, as though the universe keeps receipts for misery. You wait for your pain to qualify you for peace, but healing doesn't work like that. No amount of self-inflicted sadness can rewrite what's already over. At some point, you have to stop grieving the old version of yourself and start mentoring the new one.

Eventually, you learn that the opposite of punishment is responsibility. Real accountability says, Yes, I failed, and now I'll do better. Self-punishment says, I failed, so I'll keep suffering. One leads forward; the other keeps you circling the same shame. The strength you seek does not come from enduring pain, but from growing out of it.

How Shame Spreads

Shame rarely stays contained. It leaks into every part of life. You stop applying for things you qualify for. You hesitate to speak up in meetings. You settle for less because you think you can't handle more.

It also affects how you love. When you carry unresolved self-disappointment, you struggle to believe others can truly value you. Compliments feel dishonest. Kindness feels suspicious. You start rejecting affection before it can reject you.

Slowly, you build emotional distance to protect yourself. You tell yourself that isolation is safer than vulnerability. But what you are really doing is rehearsing rejection before it happens.

Shame convinces you that avoiding connection will prevent pain, when in truth, it only deepens loneliness.

The Work of Reclaiming Dignity

The first step to breaking shame's power is to separate identity from incident. You can acknowledge responsibility without absorbing condemnation. You can say, "I failed," and still mean, "I am not a failure."

This sounds simple, but it is not easy. The human mind does not release self-judgement quickly. You have to train it slowly, repeatedly, and deliberately.

Rebuilding dignity begins with perspective. You remind yourself that one chapter cannot define an entire book. You train your thoughts to see failure as an event, not a verdict.

You also learn to catch your self-talk before it becomes cruel. Every time you start to say, "I'm useless," you pause and correct it to "I made a mistake, and I'm learning." That small change is discipline. It is the act of teaching your brain a new language.

Over time, the tone of your inner voice changes. It becomes less like an accuser and more like a guide. That doesn't happen overnight, but it does happen.

Reclaiming dignity also means giving yourself permission to begin small again. After failure, you often want to prove your worth through big wins, but the real healing happens in consistent effort. It is in showing up for your tasks, keeping promises to yourself, and finishing what you start. Small acts of integrity rebuild self-trust. Every time you keep a word to yourself, you send a message to your mind: I can rely on myself again.

You also have to unlearn the belief that confidence only comes after success. Sometimes, you have to borrow confidence from your discipline. You act as if you believe in yourself until belief catches up. You do not wait to feel ready before rebuilding; you rebuild so that readiness can return.

And finally, you learn that dignity is not performance. It is not the image you show others when you've recovered; it is the gentle way you carry yourself while still becoming whole. You hold your head high because you have stopped apologising for being in progress. Dignity in this case is like a calm assurance that says, I fell, I learnt, and I'm still here.

Healing from shame is not a dramatic breakthrough. It is the morning you wake up and do not immediately think about the past. It is the conversation you have without pretending to be perfect. It is the moment you stop introducing yourself through apology.

It is not about forgetting what happened; it is about outgrowing its power over you.

True healing comes when you stop trying to erase the version of yourself that failed and start integrating it. You begin to see that person as a teacher, rather than a stain. You stop asking, Why did this happen to me? And start asking, What did this teach me about me?

Forgiving yourself doesn't mean you are proud of what happened. It means you are finally ready to stop being defined by it.

The Small Shifts That Matter

In time, I learnt that the opposite of shame is not pride; it is honesty. Pride hides behind perfection. Honesty stands in the open, unashamed of imperfection.

You cannot heal what you refuse to name. The act of saying, "Yes, I failed, and I'm still worthy of progress," is itself a declaration of freedom.

I began to realise that people rarely remember our failures as vividly as we do. The world forgets more quickly than shame does. While you are still replaying the moment, others have moved on to their concerns. Most of the judgement you fear lives only in your imagination.

That realisation shifted something inside me. I understood that I had been carrying shame longer than anyone expected me to.

The real danger of failure is not the fall; it is remaining loyal to your lowest moment. At some point, you have to stop returning to the ruins just to prove that you've learnt your lesson. Growth means walking forward, not circling the same memory.

Sometimes, the hardest forgiveness is granting it to yourself when no one is asking you to. You do not need to rewrite history to deserve peace. You only need to accept it as part of your becoming.

Reflection Section: A Moment to Pause

- What is the harshest thing you regularly say to yourself, and where did that voice learn its tone?
- Do you confuse accountability with self-punishment? What would healthy responsibility look like instead?
- If you separated your identity from your past mistake, what truth about yourself would remain?
- Which part of your story do you keep revisiting, and what might happen if you let it rest?
- What would your inner voice sound like if it spoke to you as kindly as you speak to others?
- What small decision this week could prove to you that you are no longer defined by disappointment?

—— Chapter Five: ——
The Work of Becoming

"Your task is not to foresee the future, but to enable it."
Antoine de Saint-Exupéry

There is a discreet moment after the storm when you begin to rebuild, not because you feel ready, but because you know staying still will only deepen the wound. At first, everything feels mechanical. You wake up, do what needs to be done, go through the motions, and try not to think too deeply. But somewhere between the repetition and the reflection, you begin to feel life return.

That is how becoming begins, not in clarity, but in motion.

The truth is, healing never announces itself. It does not come as a single day of enlightenment or an emotional breakthrough. It comes in the small choices you make to keep showing up. In those moments, you decide not to give up again. It is in the efforts you put into becoming someone trustworthy to yourself.

After my failure, I did not wake up one day full of resolve. I simply got tired of feeling stuck. I started by doing the small things I once avoided: waking early, reading again, organising my thoughts, and asking questions I was once too proud to ask. It wasn't glamorous. No one was watching. There was no applause. But it was real. And slowly, that consistency became my strength.

It took time to realise that becoming is work. It is not a poetic idea or a beautiful metaphor. It is daily, deliberate, and sometimes boring labour. It is building habits before you feel inspired. It is forgiving yourself for slipping and trying again the next morning. It is choosing progress over performance.

People often expect transformation to be dramatic. We imagine new beginnings with grand gestures, quitting jobs, moving cities, and changing everything. But in reality, becoming again rarely looks like that. It is almost always solemn.

It is the discipline of the ordinary. It is the routine that doesn't make the news but shapes your days. It is doing the right thing when no one claps for it.

There were days I studied for hours and remembered nothing. Days I woke up early, opened my notes, and stared blankly at them. There were moments I questioned whether my efforts even mattered. But consistency taught me something inspiration never could, which is that growth is not about how you feel; it is about what you keep doing despite how you feel.

Some people wait for motivation before they move. But motivation is unreliable. It is like the weather; it changes without notice. Discipline, however, is climate. It sustains you through the unpredictable days. It gives you stability when your emotions fluctuate.

When you start doing small things like reading, planning, praying, and resting faithfully, they begin to add up. The mind regains focus. The body learns balance. The heart starts to trust itself again.

There is a strange pressure today to "figure it all out". We are surrounded by highlight reels and success stories, and it feels like everyone has a grand plan. But the truth is, most progress is built on small steps.

Becoming is more about knowing the next right thing than having everything mapped out. You do not have to fix your entire life in a month. You just need to keep showing up for the day in front of you. You wake up, do what matters, and rest. The rest will unfold with time.

Starting Over Without Starting Late

For a long time, I believed that starting over meant I had lost time. It was easy to think that life had moved on without me and that my peers had gone ahead while I was still trying to rebuild.

But with time, I learnt that "late" is just a social invention. Nobody is late in a journey that has no universal clock. We all begin at different points because we all learn different lessons. Some lessons cannot be learnt early; they require detours.

Starting over is proof of endurance. Anyone can start once, but it takes courage to start again.

I remember walking through the Lagos State University gates for my second admission. The environment felt familiar yet new. I was older, humble, and far more aware of the weight of opportunity. My first instinct was to compare myself to everyone else those ahead, those my age, and those already "doing better". But I reminded myself that my race was different now. I was no longer trying to impress anyone. I was building something internal with focus, responsibility, and conviction.

The beauty of beginning again is that you carry wisdom into your new chapter. One of my mentors told me that I should never count my lost years as a waste because the lessons are already built in. In fact, he said I should see myself as someone with one degree already. You may have lost time, but you gained perspective. You now know what to avoid, what to prioritise, and what truly matters.

So, starting again is not a step backwards; it is a step forward, just taken from a humbler place.

Building Leverage

When I started again, I carried a different level of determination. I knew I couldn't rewrite the past, but I could prepare for the future differently. I didn't want to just pass through school; I wanted to become valuable.

That thought became my anchor. While others waited for opportunities, I decided to build leverage. Leverage is what happens when you stop waiting to be chosen and start choosing yourself. It is the art of multiplying your effort through learning, discipline, and self-awareness.

During my first year, I began learning digital skills like data analytics, digital marketing, communication, and anything that could give me leverage in the labour market. I didn't have much guidance at the time. Most of what I learnt came from free resources. There were nights when the process felt pointless, but deep down, I knew that knowledge is never wasted.

At first, the skills didn't pay off. I applied for internships and heard nothing back. I sent proposals, wrote cold emails, joined online programmes, and kept receiving rejection after rejection. It was humbling. But it also strengthened me. Every "no" became practice. Every rejection kept me hopeful for the time I would get an acceptance.

I realised that the world rarely rewards effort immediately. It rewards consistency. It rewards the person who stays long enough to outgrow early invisibility.

Building leverage became a kind of redemption. It made me see that my "lost time" wasn't really lost, and I could still catch up. I was learning skills and building an identity for myself. I was learning how to create value even when no one was watching.

That is what leverage does: it gives you control over your pace. It allows you to shape your growth from the inside out. When you become skilled, disciplined, and adaptable, time stops feeling like an enemy. You stop asking, How do I catch up? And start asking, How do I build forward?

Eventually, opportunities began to open, and I was ready for them.

Leverage is the bridge between recovery and relevance. It is how you redeem time that once felt wasted through the transformation of every lesson, skill, and failure into competence. You may have started late, but if you learn strategically, you can grow faster than those who never had to start over.

When Growth Becomes Gentle

There is a gentleness that comes after deep failure. You stop mocking others for their mistakes because you have felt how heavy it is to fall. You stop rushing people through their pain because you have learnt that healing cannot be timed.

That gentleness becomes one of your greatest strengths. It makes you patient with others but even more patient with yourself.

Becoming again makes you softer without losing strength. It helps you find balance and to remain firm in conviction, yet kind in expression.

With time, I learnt to speak to myself differently. I no longer used harsh language when I made small mistakes. I didn't overanalyse every failure. I simply said, "We'll do better tomorrow," and meant it.

The Work Beneath the Work

People often focus on external progress like new grades, new jobs, and new accomplishments, but the deeper work of becoming happens beneath the surface. It happens in the mind.

You start unlearning old beliefs that your worth depends on achievement, that mistakes erase value, and that people's opinions define your direction. You start recognising that peace is internal, not circumstantial.

The hardest part is retraining your thoughts. You can't build a new life with an old mindset. You have to learn to think like someone who deserves peace, not punishment.

There were moments I had to remind myself that discipline is not cruelty. Rest is not laziness. Progress is not linear. Those small shifts in thinking made it possible to sustain change.

That is the work beneath the work, rebuilding the inner architecture of your mind so that you no longer sabotage what you are praying for.

But this inner transformation also changes how you relate to people. When your mind becomes healthier, you stop depending on validation to feel whole. You begin to speak from surety, not from insecurity. You listen differently, not to defend yourself, but to understand.

The work beneath the work also means being honest about your triggers. You start to recognise patterns, the same habits that lead to exhaustion, the same thoughts that feed self-doubt, and the same distractions that delay growth. You stop pretending not to see them and begin to address them. This is what true awareness looks like: seeing clearly without condemning yourself for what you see.

And slowly, you notice that your reactions change. You no longer rush decisions just to dismiss anxiety. You no longer seek noise to escape silence. You begin to live deliberately. That shift does not make life perfect, but it makes you stable.

The Patience of Becoming

We are conditioned to chase outcomes. We want visible results, measurable wins, and quick transformations, but becoming again requires patience, the kind that feels endless but builds endurance.

Patience is not passive waiting; it is active trust. It's doing your share while acknowledging that time has its own role to play.

I used to rush everything. I wanted to prove that I had bounced back quickly, that I was strong. But rushing only repeated the same mistakes: burnout, comparison, and anxiety.

Patience teaches you humility. You start to understand that timing is not something you control; it is something you cooperate with. There is a difference between movement and maturity. Movement happens fast, but maturity takes time. You learn to respect divine timing, the unseen order that arranges things in ways your urgency never could. What looks like a delay often turns out to be protection or preparation.

There were seasons when I felt forgotten, but those were the seasons that refined me. Waiting stripped away my pride and forced me to confront who I was when no one was watching. That is what patience really does: it reveals the truth of your character. Anyone can stay disciplined when the reward is visible; it takes deeper strength to remain faithful when there is no applause.

Patience also simplifies life. When you stop demanding results immediately, you start focusing on process. You begin to see growth as something organic, not mechanical. You stop rushing to harvest and start paying attention to the soil (your habits, your thoughts, your prayers, and your relationships). You realise that the person you are becoming matters more than the milestones you reach.

And perhaps the most beautiful thing about patience is how it changes your relationship with time itself. You stop counting months and start counting lessons. You stop envying those ahead and start learning from where you stand. You begin to see that growth is not something you chase; it is something you grow into, one day at a time.

A Verse for the Journey

In the Qur'an, there is a verse that says, "Indeed, Allah will not change the condition of a people until they change what is in themselves." It reminds me that renewal is never external first. It begins with the invisible decisions to think better, to speak better, and to act better, even when no one notices.

That verse is a promise that the power to change is never beyond your reach.

Looking back, I realise that becoming again was a series of small moments. That is the true work of becoming—the work that is unseen, persistent, and only you recognise and celebrate.

And if you stay with it long enough, one day you'll wake up and realise that the version of you that once felt broken has become the version of you that others draw strength from. You won't even notice the exact moment it happened.

Reflection Section: A Moment to Pause

- What small discipline are you neglecting that could help rebuild your confidence?
- How can you make peace with the pace of your process?
- Which habits remind you that growth doesn't need an audience?
- What does "starting over" mean to you now: punishment or privilege?
- In what area of your life are you still performing instead of becoming?
- How can you practise gentleness without losing responsibility?
- What would it look like to live in peace instead of under pressure this week?

—— Chapter Six: ——
When Control Slips Away

"You planned, and Allah planned. And Allah is the best of planners." Qur'an 3:54

There comes a point in every life when your plans no longer obey you. You did everything right, worked hard, stayed careful, and made the right choices, but still, things fall apart. It doesn't always happen in one moment. Sometimes, it is gradual. You begin to notice that the world no longer bends to your effort. You lose your grip, little by little, until you realise that the control you thought you had was never really yours.

At first, it feels terrifying. We have been taught to believe that control is safety and that life can be managed like a project. We make vision boards, write goals, draw timelines, and convince ourselves that diligence guarantees direction. But then life interrupts the script. Something breaks. Something shifts. You fail. You lose something you thought was secure. You realise that effort is not ownership.

That realisation hurts because control gives us the illusion of certainty. It tells us that if we do enough, plan enough, or believe enough, we can predict outcomes. But the truth is harder: life is not an equation; it is a conversation. And sometimes, it speaks in ways that force you to listen.

We live in a generation obsessed with mastery. We want to master productivity, relationships, and even spirituality. We build systems and routines, seeking security in perfection. We treat control like a virtue. But the more you try to master everything, the more you realise that mastery has limits. You can plan your time, but you cannot plan your timing. You can manage your emotions, but not what triggers them. You can work on your dreams but not decide when they will manifest. At some point, life will interrupt you so that you will understand that growth cannot be engineered.

There was a season when I tried to control my routine, my studies, and my outcomes. I thought if I just worked hard enough, I could force things to go right. But control slowly turned into anxiety. I was constantly on alert, waiting for things to go wrong. I couldn't rest because I feared rest would make me lose momentum. When life eventually disrupted my plans, I was angry. I called it unfair. But in hindsight, it was mercy. It was an invitation to humility and, more importantly, a reminder that I am human, not a machine.

Beneath our obsession with control lies the gentle voice of ego. The belief that we are strong enough to hold the universe together if we just try harder. We do not usually call it ego because it hides behind responsibility and ambition. But it is the ego that tells us we can outthink disappointment. It is the ego that panics when things do not go according to plan. It is the ego that whispers, I must fix this before anyone sees me fail.

Failure exposes that illusion. It humbles us into realising that control was never strength; surrender is. When things start slipping away, the ego resists. It tightens its grip, doubles its effort, and tries to pretend that nothing is wrong. But the more you resist, the more life pushes back. Until finally, you stop fighting, and something beautiful happens: peace. You realise that surrender is not weakness. It is the moment you stop trying to play God and start trusting life again.

Every failure, every disappointment, every unexpected pause carries a hidden invitation. It asks, Will you let this teach you something, or will you let it break you? For me, that invitation came the moment I realised my plans were not working. I had done everything "right". I had been focused, prayerful, and careful. Yet the outcome was not what I expected. At first, I was frustrated. I wanted answers. I wanted explanations that made sense. But sometimes, the meaning doesn't come immediately. Sometimes, all you receive is silence. And in that silence, you begin to see the real lesson: that control is not the same as stability.

True stability comes from adaptability, not predictability. It is not about knowing what will happen next; it is about knowing that you will still be okay when it does. That is what surrender teaches you. That peace does not depend on having control but on learning to flow with life instead of fighting it. There are seasons when life rearranges itself without your permission. The job ends. The friendship fades. The opportunity you thought was yours slips away. You feel betrayed by the very effort that was meant to protect you. But every interruption carries meaning. It forces you to ask: Who am I without my plans?

That question is uncomfortable, but it is salient and sacred. It peels away the layers of identity you built around productivity and reputation. It reveals the part of you that existed before success, before titles, and before performance. When control slips away, what is left is the truth—raw, humbling, sometimes painful, but always cleansing. It is in those moments that you discover how much of your confidence was circumstantial. You realise that many of the things you thought defined you were just accessories to your identity. And when they fall away, you meet yourself again, bare, but real.

There is a verse in the Qur'an that says, "Perhaps you dislike a thing and it is good for you, and perhaps you love a thing and it is bad for you. And Allah knows, while you know not." That verse used to frustrate me because it demands trust without full understanding. But over time, I learnt that it is not asking for blind faith; it is asking for wisdom. It is teaching that some interruptions are actually instructions. Some endings are not punishment but protection. When control slips away, faith becomes the ability to breathe in uncertainty and still believe that something purposeful is unfolding. You learn to say, This didn't go my way, but maybe it is still going the right way. That single shift in perspective can turn chaos into clarity.

There is a kind of peace that only comes when you stop insisting on how life should look. You begin to see that the need to control everything is rooted in fear. Fear of loss, fear of embarrassment, fear of uncertainty. But fear cannot coexist with peace. The moment you loosen your grip, you realise you were never holding much anyway. Life has always had a rhythm to it. Your plans were just temporary maps, useful but not absolute. This doesn't mean you stop planning or caring. It means you stop panicking when life rearranges what you planned. It means you start trusting that growth sometimes looks like a detour.

When you release control, you begin to notice life's intelligence, how things you once begged to keep would have limited you, and how what you resisted losing made room for what you actually needed. Surrender purifies ambition. It separates desire from desperation. It turns your drive inward to control your response and not the outcome. When you finally accept that control is an illusion, you stop forcing your story and start listening to it. You stop rushing through seasons and start learning from them. You stop performing strength and start practising peace.

In surrender, you become softer, not weaker but wiser. You stop seeing detours as enemies and start recognising them as mirrors. Each one reflects a part of you that still needs humility, faith, or patience. That is how failure becomes both a teacher and a mirror, not because it ruins your plans, but because it reveals your attachments. It shows you what you fear losing most and calls you to hold it more loosely.

When control slips away, life is inviting you. Inviting you to see yourself clearly, to grow beyond your ego, and to let go of the illusion that certainty equals peace. There is a peace that control can never give, the peace that comes from trust. Trust in the process. Trust in timing. Trust in your ability to adapt. You may never fully stop planning, but you can plan with open hands instead of clenched fists.

And one day, when life interrupts you again, because it will, maybe you won't panic. You might stop, take a deep breath, and murmur, "Maybe this, too, is becoming."

Reflection Section: A Moment to Pause

- What part of your life do you still feel the need to control, and why?
- What would happen if you loosened your grip just a little?
- How does your ego react when things do not go according to plan?
- Which recent interruption in your life might actually be an invitation to grow?
- What does surrender mean to you?
- How can you start trusting timing without losing effort?

——Chapter Seven:——
The Mirror Called Failure

"Success is often built on a mountain of failures."
Raymond Reddington

Failure has a way of holding a mirror to your face that success never will. Mirrors don't lie or flatter, and they don't wait for your permission. They simply reflect what they have ahead of them. It shows you everything you have ignored: your fears, your motives, your attachments, and your illusions. It forces you to confront who you really are when the applause fades and the plans collapse.

Most people fear failure because they think it will ruin their image. What they do not realise is that failure doesn't destroy identity; it reveals it. It strips away the layers of pretence and shows you whether what you believed about yourself was built on truth or ego.

When I failed, I thought the worst part was losing direction, but what hurt more was losing the version of myself I thought I was. I had believed I was disciplined, consistent, and responsible, but suddenly the evidence said otherwise. It felt like the mirror was mocking me. But in time, I understood that the mirror was actually clarifying my true colour. Failure was not saying, You are not who you thought you were. It was saying, You are not yet who you think you are.

That difference changed everything.

Failure is not just an event; it is an X-ray. It reveals where strength was genuine and where it was borrowed. It exposes what you built out of conviction and what you built for validation. It shows you which parts of you were built to last and which were only holding because no one had tested them yet.

In that sense, failure is one of the most honest friends you will ever have, but only if you are brave enough to accept it.

At first, I tried to look away. I tried to hide behind productivity, telling myself that if I just moved fast enough, I could outrun the shame. But failure doesn't disappear when you ignore it; it waits. It lingers in your serene moments, asking the same questions repeatedly. And if you do not face them, you repeat them.

That is why some people go from one mistake to another that looks different but feels the same. This is because they never looked long enough into the mirror to see what needed changing. They cleaned the surface but never dealt with the reflection.

The mirror of failure doesn't only show where you fell short; it shows why. It reveals the habits you have ignored, the pride you have justified, and the fears you have decorated with ambition. It exposes how much of your drive was rooted in proving, not becoming.

For me, it exposed my obsession with control, how much I had built my worth on achievement, and how quickly I lost confidence when that achievement disappeared. I realised that I was working under pressure. My effort was not always sincere; it was sometimes fuelled by fear. Failure forced me to see that, and it was uncomfortable.

There is a unique humiliation in watching your ego crumble. You start to see how dependent you were on outcomes for identity. You start to notice how much energy went into being seen as "put together". You realise that many of your goals were more about perception than about purpose.

That realisation can either break or free you.

When you finally accept that your worth is not tied to your performance, failure becomes less frightening. It becomes feedback. It stops being a sentence and becomes a conversation. You start to listen differently and reflect more deeply.

The truth is, failure is only shameful if you refuse to learn from it. If you allow it to teach you, it becomes sacred. It becomes a spiritual tool, whether you are religious or not, because it humbles you into self-awareness.

In the silence that follows disappointment, you start to hear your real motives. You begin to ask deeper questions. Why did I want that so badly? Who was I trying to impress? What part of me felt incomplete without that success? Those questions are uncomfortable, but they are the birthplace of authenticity.

Many people spend their lives chasing achievements without ever confronting those questions. Failure forces you to stop and look inward. It disrupts the performance so you meet your true self. And that encounter, though painful, is transformative.

When you see yourself clearly, you begin to understand others differently. You stop judging people for falling short because you now understand how easy it is to do so. You become slower to criticise, quicker to listen, and more forgiving, because you have tasted humility.

That humility doesn't make you smaller; it makes you real. It gives you balance. You no longer need to prove your intelligence, your worth, or your discipline. You simply focus on doing the work internally, knowing that depth is more valuable than display.

Failure also teaches you emotional honesty. It shows you how to sit with discomfort without trying to escape it. We live in a time when people fear silence, and distraction has become a form of therapy. But failure forces stillness. It teaches you to stay with pain long enough to hear what it is saying.

I learnt that some forms of discomfort are not meant to be avoided; they are meant to be listened to. The sting of failure often points to areas for growth. The guilt you feel after disappointment is often a sign that your standards are alive. Even shame can serve a purpose when you respond with curiosity instead of condemnation.

That is what makes failure a mirror; it reflects the state of your inner world. It shows you what you worship, what you fear, and what you need to unlearn. It reveals whether you are building your life on ego or on essence.

Sometimes, it takes losing everything that validated you to finally recognise what is real in you.

I think that is why failure hurts so deeply, because it exposes our dependence on fragile things. When those things are stripped away, you face the question of who you really are. And if you can sit in that question long enough, something remarkable happens: you begin to discover a self that doesn't crumble under uncertainty. The version of you that cannot be bribed by praise or destroyed by loss. The version of you that knows peace is internal, not performative.

When I began to rebuild my confidence, I did it differently. I no longer wanted perfection; I wanted honesty. I didn't need to be the best anymore; I just needed to be true. I stopped performing resilience and started practising it. I stopped quoting strength and started living it.

Failure taught me that authenticity is harder than achievement. It is easier to chase success than to confront yourself. But once you learn honesty, you begin to live lighter. You stop negotiating your worth with outcomes. You stop explaining your journey to people who never carry your context. You stop apologising for evolving.

There is a subtle power in people who have failed deeply and learnt from it. They move differently. They do not panic when plans shift. They do not chase attention. They know that peace is more valuable than perfection. They have seen life's unpredictability and stopped trying to control it.

And yet, the beauty of failure is that it doesn't just reveal; it refines. It takes the raw material of your character and burns away the excess. It teaches discernment. You stop wasting energy on the unnecessary. You start building your life on things that can survive reality.

You become more intentional about who you keep close, how you spend your time, and what kind of peace you protect. You no longer chase busy days; you choose meaningful ones. You no longer crave being seen everywhere; you focus on being present where it matters.

In that way, failure becomes a kind of fire that purifies. It burns away the illusions, leaving you with the essence. You begin to see that your value never depended on performance; it was always tied to presence. And perhaps that is the most important lesson of all: what breaks you can also build you if you stop resisting it.

That realisation calmed me. It made me stop asking, "Why me?" and start asking, "What is this trying to teach me?" And slowly, failure became less of a curse and more of a compass. Every setback now carries direction. Every closed door whispers correction. Every loss comes with a revelation.

The mirror called failure is not cruel; it is honest. It doesn't punish you; it prepares you. It invites you to release the image you were chasing and return to the essence you had forgotten.

And if you can stand before that mirror, trembling, uncertain, but willing to see, you will find that what you lost was never the point. What you discovered within yourself was.

Reflection Section: A Moment to Pause

- What truth about yourself did failure reveal that success never could?
- How do you respond when the mirror of disappointment shows you something uncomfortable?
- In what ways have you confused performance with purpose in your life?
- What would it mean to rebuild your worth on honesty instead of achievement?
- How has failure refined the person you are becoming?

—— Chapter Eight: ——
The Ego That Breaks Before You Do

"Indeed, Allah does not love the arrogant and boastful."
Qur'an 31:18

There is a breaking that happens long before life breaks you, the slow cracking of the ego. It is the moment you realise you are not as in control or as invincible as you once believed. It slips in through humiliations and moments where you are forced to meet your humanity.

Ego doesn't announce itself. It wears disguises of confidence, ambition, and even humility. It hides behind your best traits, feeding off the very things that make you admirable. It convinces you that self-importance is self-respect and that being right is equivalent to being wise. For a long time, you carry it unknowingly, mistaking it for strength.

Then failure comes, and the disguise falls apart.

When the things you built your worth around begin to crumble, you realise how fragile pride really is. The ego is loud when life is going well, but the moment things fall apart, it becomes desperate. It looks for someone to blame, something to prove, or a way to pretend that nothing is wrong. That is what makes failure so devastating. The preconceived illusion that you were ever above falling is what makes the fall more painful.

I used to think confidence meant being unshakeable, always composed, always right, and always ready. But real confidence comes from knowing you do not need to be perfect to be at peace. Ego demands control, but confidence accepts growth.

Ego thrives on appearance. It feeds on comparison, applause, and recognition. It convinces you that you must constantly improve, stay ahead, and be strong. But life has a way of humbling you into stillness. When things stop working, when progress slows, when validation dries up, ego panics. It doesn't know how to exist without proof of worth. That is where humility begins.

Humility is not weakness. It is clarity, the clear-eyed understanding that you are human, that life owes you nothing, and that everything you have is both a gift and a responsibility.

When the ego breaks, what is left is truth. You stop needing to be perceived as special and start focusing on being sincere. You stop rushing to speak and begin to listen. You stop trying to win arguments and start trying to understand. It's a subtle way of living, but it is infinitely more peaceful.

Ryan Holiday, in Ego Is the Enemy, writes that "the greatest impediment to success is not failure but our ego." That line stopped me the first time I read it. Because it explained what I couldn't yet name: that sometimes, the real danger is not falling short, but becoming full of yourself when you succeed. Ego blinds you to the work of mastery because it tells you that you have already arrived.

Holiday speaks of the three stages of ego: when we aspire, when we succeed, and when we fail. Each stage tests us differently. When we aspire, the ego makes us impatient; we want the results before we have done the work. When we succeed, ego tempts us to believe the praise. And when we fail, ego whispers that we've lost everything, that we are nothing without what we built.

I experienced all three phases in my life. When I was pursuing success, I sought quick fixes and small wins that would demonstrate my abilities. When I finally made progress, I became careless, believing effort alone would keep me afloat. But when I failed, I convinced myself that I had been permanently disqualified. In all three stages, the voice behind it was the same, but the ego was dressed differently each time.

Ego tells you you are always the exception. Humility reminds you that you are still a student of life.

Holiday says, "Always stay a student." It is such a simple sentence, yet so difficult to live. Because ego resists being taught. It believes learning is for those who do not know enough, forgetting that wisdom begins where certainty ends.

When your ego breaks, you rediscover the joy of learning. You start reading differently, not to sound informed, but to understand. You start listening to people you once overlooked. You stop defending your mistakes and start learning from them. You accept correction without collapsing.

The irony is that when you finally let go of the need to be important, you begin to do work that truly matters. You stop chasing recognition and start chasing meaning. You begin to see that greatness has nothing to do with attention. As Holiday wrote, "Impressing people is utterly different from being truly impressive."

That distinction changes everything.

The ego is obsessed with being seen; humility wants to be useful. Ego wants to be right; humility seeks to be real. Ego seeks the spotlight; humility builds the foundation.

The day you stop performing for approval, you start working for purpose. That shift will definitely alter the course of your life.

When you begin to live in humility, you realise that progress is not linear, and that is okay. You become patient with your becoming. You understand that growth doesn't have to be visible to be valid. You stop rushing seasons that were designed to teach you endurance.

And slowly, the noise fades. You become anchored again, not in outcomes, but in values.

The Qur'an says, "Do not walk upon the earth with arrogance; indeed, you can neither pierce the earth nor reach the mountains in height." It serves as a reminder that, no matter how far we progress, we will always be human, fragile, dependent, and small in the vastness of creation. This truth rescues you from the illusion that everything revolves around your effort.

When the ego breaks, gratitude takes its place. You begin to see that not everything you lost was punishment; some things were pruning. Not every closed door was rejection; some were protection. You stop trying to manage outcomes and start managing your responses.

That is where maturity begins, in the acceptance that you can be enough and still have room to grow. You can be talented and still need correction. You can be confident and still need guidance.

Ryan Holiday calls this "the canvas" strategy, the idea that sometimes, the most powerful way to grow is to help others paint their masterpiece. To make yourself useful instead of visible. To stop obsessing about how to be noticed and instead focus on how to contribute.

When your ego breaks, you start living like that. You begin to see leadership not as hierarchy but as service. You start showing up not to prove your brilliance but to support the mission. That change makes you significant in a lasting way.

Ego builds empires; humility builds legacies.

You realise that real power is not in being above people but in being rooted among them, grounded, compassionate, and teachable.

Sometimes, I think failure's greatest mercy is that it breaks the ego before it destroys the person. Because if you never fall, you start believing you are untouchable. You become careless with others, yourself, and with grace. You start mistaking privilege for entitlement and gifts for guarantees. But when failure arrives, it dismantles the illusion. It saves you from a worse fall, the one that pride would have led you to.

There is a particular peace that comes after the ego dies, a stillness that doesn't crave validation. You stop chasing applause because you have learnt how fleeting it is. You start cherishing moments instead of milestones. You begin to measure your worth not by what you have achieved, but by how much you've grown in patience, empathy, and integrity.

That is when you begin to live truly free.

When the ego breaks, you no longer need to win every

argument. You no longer need to be the loudest in the room. You can let others shine because their light doesn't dim yours. You begin to see life as collaboration, not competition.

The work you do from that place carries a different weight. It is steady, pure, and peaceful.

Ryan Holiday writes, "Ego is the enemy of what you want and of what you have: of mastery, of staying at the top, of creativity, and of working well with others." The truth of that line is everywhere around us. You can see it in broken teams, fragile leaders, and people who had everything but couldn't sustain peace. Ego builds fast but breaks easily.

But when you let it go, when you truly let it break before you do, you start to experience a different kind of power, the power of self-awareness. You become less reactive and more intentional. You no longer need to prove your worth; you embody it. You walk lighter. You breathe easier. You begin to see that humility is not the opposite of strength but its foundation.

When you let the ego break before you do, you find the version of you that can finally live without armour.

Reflection Section: A Moment to Pause

- What part of your ego resists being perceived as "in progress"?
- Where in your life are you chasing visibility instead of value?
- What would it look like to "stay a student" even in your moments of success?
- How has failure saved you from pride you didn't know you had?
- Who could you serve as part of your becoming?

——Chapter Nine:——
Falling Without Shame

"Do not lose hope, nor be sad."
Qur'an 3:139

Failure has a way of introducing you to yourself. Not the version that people clap for, but the one who sits alone after the noise fades, the one who wrestles with silence and regret, the one who learns how to breathe through disappointment. When I fell, it wasn't the failure itself that hurt the most; it was the shame that followed.

Shame is modest but brutal. It doesn't just say, "You did something wrong." It whispers, "You are something wrong." It stains every memory of effort and wraps every intention in doubt. I carried shame like a second skin for weeks after I found out that I had been advised to withdraw. It followed me everywhere. Even my reflection felt like a witness against me.

You see, no one teaches you how to fall with dignity. In school, family, and society, we are taught to strive, succeed, and maintain face. We are told to make our parents proud, our teachers pleased, and our peers impressed. But no one tells you what to do when you fall short. No one says how to carry failure without losing yourself. And so, when it happens, we assume that failure means we have become less human. We withdraw. We shrink. We disappear.

But silence is deceptive. It pretends to protect you while it secretly isolates you. I thought hiding would spare me from judgement, but it only made my thoughts louder. The mind is not merciful when left alone too long. You start inventing conversations that never happened, imagining the words people might say if they knew your truth. Soon, the punishment you fear from others becomes the punishment you deliver to yourself.

Brené Brown once wrote that shame is the fear of disconnection. It is the belief that something we have done makes us unworthy of love and belonging. That is exactly how it felt. I did not fear the result itself as much as I feared what people would now think of me. Every time someone asked how I was doing, I felt the question as an accusation. When someone encouraged me, I wondered if they were only being kind because they pitied me. I couldn't bear the thought of being "that student", the one who lost it all.

However, time has taught me that shame does not tell the truth. It tells the version of the story that never ends in redemption. It is a narrative that stops before grace has a chance to enter.

The first step toward falling without shame is learning to tell the story differently. Instead of "I failed because I'm not enough," you learn to say, "I failed because I'm learning." Instead of "I disappointed everyone," you begin to say, "I am discovering what matters to me." This shift doesn't happen overnight. It happens through a gentle retraining of your inner voice.

The story we tell ourselves after failure decides how long we stay broken. For some people, the story becomes a scar they touch every day to remember their pain. For others, it becomes a map that guides them toward self-awareness. You get to choose which one yours will be. The story itself doesn't change; what changes is the meaning you attach to it. Healing begins when you stop using your story as evidence against yourself.

James Clear, in his book Atomic Habits, says that every action is a vote for the type of person you want to become. The same is true for how we speak to ourselves. Every word we use to describe our failure is a vote for how we will recover from it. Shame says, "I'm broken." Growth says, "I'm being rebuilt."

When you fall without shame, you stop confusing your mistakes with your identity. You start seeing failure as a moment, not a label. You begin to look at your life as a story that is still being written.

For a long time, I replayed my failure like a loop: the day the news was delivered, the walk back to the hostel, and the sleepless nights that followed. But somewhere in that period, I realised that I wasn't mourning only the failure; I was mourning the image I had of myself. I had tied my self-worth to my performance. Once that collapsed, I didn't know who I was.

That is when Viktor Frankl's words began to make sense to me. In Man's Search for Meaning, he wrote that those who have a "why" can bear almost any "how". It took me months to see it, but the fall had stripped me of every "why" I thought I had: approval, perfection, and reputation, and left me empty enough to find a real one. The pain wasn't pointless; it was redirecting me toward purpose.

Purpose doesn't erase failure. It redeems it.

In time, I realised that the fall had stripped me of vanity. It taught me that humility is not thinking less of yourself but thinking of yourself truthfully. I stopped trying to appear strong and started learning what real strength felt like, the subtle kind, built in the privacy of ordinary days. Some mornings, all I managed was to show up and try again. But even that, I learnt, was sacred work. Trying again is one of the most sacred forms of faith.

When Anne Lamott said, "Perfectionism is the voice of the oppressor," she was right. I spent too long performing competence instead of practising growth. I thought that if I could appear fine, I would become fine. But pretence only delays progress. True healing begins where pretending ends.

There is a subtle bravery in showing up as you are, flawed, unfinished, but willing. It is not glamorous, and it doesn't make for an inspiring social media post. But it is the only way transformation happens.

Carol Dweck's research on growth mindset helped me put language to this. According to her, people with a fixed mindset view failure as the ultimate measure of ability, whereas those with a growth mindset see it as information. The difference between shame and learning is interpretation. Shame ends the sentence; learning continues it.

When you decide to fall without shame, you give yourself permission to continue the sentence. You start asking, What can this teach me? What can I do differently? What part of me needed this lesson?

I sometimes believe that the most honest feedback loop in life is failure. It reveals false beliefs about control, entitlement, effort, and reward that we were unaware we held. It forces us to confront the fact that we are not the sum of our wins. We are the sum of our courage to keep showing up.

That shift changes everything. You begin to measure progress differently. You start to celebrate small, internal victories: the day you forgive yourself a little more easily, the morning you wake up without the weight of regret, and the moment you realise you no longer flinch at your reflection. These are the milestones of someone learning to fall without shame.

Parker Palmer wrote, "Wholeness does not mean perfection. It means embracing brokenness as an integral part of life." That line stayed with me because it captures the essence of this journey. Falling without shame doesn't mean pretending the fall never happened. It means acknowledging it without self-destruction. It means saying, I am not defined by the fall; I am shaped by the rise.

C.S. Lewis once described failures as "fingerposts on the road to achievement." I used to think that was just poetic optimism. But now, I understand that those fingerposts are the directions that pain leaves behind. Failure does not mark the end of the road; rather, it directs you to a turn you may have missed.

If you allow it, failure becomes a teacher that humbles you into wisdom.

There's also something profoundly spiritual about learning to live unashamed. In the Qur'an, Allah says, "Do not despair of the mercy of Allah; indeed, Allah forgives all sins." It is a verse about hope and also about identity. It reminds you that mercy is greater than your mistakes and that your Creator defines you by potential, not by error. When you internalise that, shame loses its authority.

Still, letting go of shame doesn't mean dismissing responsibility. Accountability and shame are not the same. Accountability says, "I made a mistake, and I can correct it." Shame says, "I made a mistake, and I am a mistake." One heals; the other hardens.

You cannot carry both growth and guilt for long. One will suffocate the other. To fall without shame, you must decide which one deserves to stay.

The hardest part is choosing forgiveness when punishment feels more natural. For, a long time, I thought I needed to suffer before I could start again, as if healing had to be earned through pain. But grace is not transactional. It does not wait for you to bleed enough before it believes you have learnt your lesson. Grace meets you exactly where you fall and teaches you to rise gently. When you finally accept that, you begin to move with a new kind of confidence, the kind that no longer depends on perfection.

The older I get, the more I realise that everyone is falling somewhere. Everyone is carrying a hidden bruise, a business that failed, a relationship that ended, or a dream that didn't survive. The difference between those who rebuild and those who remain broken is not luck. It is perspective. Some see failure as proof they are cursed; others see it as evidence that they are alive.

I often think about how kindness begins with falling. The more you have failed, the softer you become with others. You stop mocking people's mistakes because you recognise yourself in them. You stop demanding perfection because you've seen how exhausting it is to chase it. Falling without shame makes you merciful. It humanises you. It refines your empathy.

It also teaches you how to rebuild slowly. You learn that progress doesn't need to be flamboyant to be real. You learn that silence can be sacred, a space for reflection, not punishment. You discover that you can walk through public places without concealing your story, because it no longer defines your worth.

One evening, I sat at my desk thinking about how much time I had wasted worrying about perception. I realised that the people whose opinions I feared most had long moved on. The only one keeping the memory alive was me. Shame, I discovered, is a ghost that lives in your mind. It feeds on imagination, not truth.

That night, I wrote a short line in my journal: "You can fall and still be loved." It was simple, but it changed everything. Every time I was tempted to withdraw, I repeated it. Every time I doubted my worth, I whispered it again. Over time, it became a belief and conviction.

When you fall without shame, you realise that survival is not the same as failure. It is proof of resilience. It is proof that you can lose something and not lose yourself.

You also begin to live differently. You become slower to judge and quicker to understand. You begin to set boundaries not out of arrogance, but from peace. You no longer crave validation because you have learnt that external approval is the cheapest kind of comfort.

Eventually, the fall that once embarrassed you becomes the story that empowers you. You begin to speak about it not with guilt, but with gratitude. You tell others that there is life after falling, just like I am doing now. This is not because it sounds wise, but because you have lived it.

One day, you will look back and realise that shame had no lasting power; it was a fog that only felt permanent because you stayed in it too long. You will laugh at how much weight you once gave to other people's opinions. You will thank the version of yourself that refused to give up, even when no one was watching. And perhaps you will start helping others climb out of their fog, reminding them that it is not weakness to fall; it is evidence that you were brave enough to move.

And maybe that is what it means to fall without shame, to stop being afraid of being recognised as human.

Because the truth is, every great life is a sequence of recoveries. You rise, you stumble, and you rise again. Falling is the process of becoming, not its antithesis. You do not graduate from imperfection. You grow with it, learning to walk taller each time, because you kept getting up.

Falling without shame is a posture. It is how you choose to stand in the world, unafraid to fail, learn, and start over.

And maybe, that is the point of it all: that grace is not found in never falling, but in realising that each time you do, you are still worthy of rising.

Reflection Section: A Moment to Pause

- What do you still feel ashamed of that you need to see as simply human?
- How much of your guilt comes from your mistake, and how much from how others might perceive it?
- What would forgiving your younger self look like today?
- How do you define responsibility without self-punishment?
- If you stopped feeling guilty about your fall, what truth would you start living differently?

—— Chapter Ten: ——
The Anatomy of Starting Over

"Every new beginning comes from some other beginning's end."
Seneca

Starting over is rarely glamorous. It is not the dramatic moment we imagine, a cinematic sunrise or a neat declaration that everything has changed. It is slower, sober, and far less certain. It often begins with a sigh. With a deep breath and a small decision whispered in the privacy of your thoughts: I will not stay here forever.

When people say, "You can always start again," they make it sound simple. But they rarely talk about the confusion that comes with it, the grief of lost time, the weight of disappointment, and the fear that maybe you have used up your chances. Starting over feels like walking barefoot across a road you once ran through confidently. You remember every step, but you no longer trust your balance.

After my withdrawal, I didn't know how to begin again. The idea of another admission, another round of lectures, and another set of faces asking, "What happened?" felt unbearable. But I realised that the longer I delayed, the heavier regret would grow. So I started small. I researched schools. I asked questions. I prayed. There was no lightning bolt of motivation, just small daily movements. That is what starting over actually looks like intentionality.

I did not feel like a phoenix when I eventually went back to school. I felt like someone sweeping the ashes. But that, too, is part of the anatomy of renewal: accepting that recovery doesn't have to look dramatic to be real.

Starting over begins with honesty. It requires you to name what broke, without bitterness, and to examine the ruins for what still holds value. Sometimes, all that remains is the will to try again. And that is enough.

T. S. Eliot once wrote, "For us, there is only the trying. The rest is not our business." Those words carried me. I had to come to understand that effort is more valuable than results. Starting over does not demand certainty. It asks for courage in uncertainty.

When I resumed, my energy was different. I was not desperate to prove myself; I was determined to be consistent. The fear of failure had lost its teeth because I had already seen what it looked like. What I wanted now was steadiness. I wanted peace more than perfection.

That shift changed everything.

It's what James Clear refers to as "identity-based habit". It means building behaviour around who you wish to become. Each morning, I reminded myself that I was not just a student; I was a steward of a second chance. That identity shaped my actions. I studied, not because I feared another failure, but because I respected the grace of being allowed to try again.

Making a fresh start is a discipline and a faith, a science and an art. The science is in the structure: how you plan, prioritise, and persist. The art is in the spirit: how you forgive, hope, and endure. Both are necessary. One without the other causes imbalance, which can result in either emotional collapse or mechanical effort.

I often tell people that failure is like falling into water.

Drowning is not inevitable; it only happens if you refuse to move. Movement is the soul of starting over. You may not swim far at first, but the act of moving keeps you alive.

There is a story I have always loved about Thomas Edison. After years of experiments and thousands of failed attempts at inventing the electric bulb, a reporter asked how it felt to fail so many times. Edison replied, "I have not failed. I have just found 10,000 ways that won't work." I used to think that quote was cliché, but now I see its humility. Edison's secret wasn't genius; it was resilience. He saw every failure as a continuation of effort, not the end of it.

The same pattern plays out in our lives, too, in people who rebuild not from laboratories but from living rooms. I once met a tailor who lost her small shop in a market fire. Everything from fabric, machines, and other materials, all gone in a night. For months, she did nothing, convinced her skill was wasted. Then one afternoon, she borrowed a friend's sewing machine and began again from her one-bedroom apartment. Today, she teaches apprentices across the city. When I asked what made her restart, she said, "The market burnt, not my hands."

Starting over is more about rediscovering what remains within you than about erasing what happened.

Viktor Frankl, who survived the horrors of concentration camps, wrote that "When we are no longer able to change a situation, we are challenged to change ourselves." Those words hold a profound truth. Sometimes, the situation cannot be fixed, the job is gone, the dream has ended, and the door has closed, but the self can be rebuilt. And that rebuilding is where all new beginnings begin.

Starting over is uncomfortable because it forces you to leave behind what is familiar, even if it no longer serves you. It demands that you walk with less certainty but more awareness. It asks for faith in motion, the kind of faith that acts even when assurance is absent.

Every comeback story has a private, unglamorous chapter where the person had to fight through monotony, long study hours, tranquil mornings, and invisible work. Progress rarely announces itself. It grows silently, like roots before a tree appears.

There is something sacred about slow progress. It breaks your attachment to applause. It teaches you to draw satisfaction from effort, not outcomes. When I studied quietly that year, there was no crowd watching and no applause. But I began to feel a new kind of peace, the kind that comes from alignment between what you believe and how you live.

Paulo Coelho wrote in The Alchemist, "When you can't go back, you have to worry only about the best way of moving forward." That sentence became my compass. I stopped trying to recreate the past. I started investing in becoming better for the future.

I have also learnt that starting over requires protecting your new beginning from old distractions. Every version of you that failed is waiting for a chance to return: the procrastination, the self-doubt, and the need to impress. If you do not stay conscious, the habits that ruined yesterday will follow you into tomorrow.

That is why reflection matters. Before you rebuild, study your collapse. Ask, What pattern brought me here? What lesson is asking to be learnt? Without that honesty, you will repeat history in a different colour.

One of my mentors once told me, "Don't rush to fix your life. First, understand how it broke." At first, I thought it sounded harsh, but I later understood. Understanding the anatomy of failure is how you design the anatomy of starting over. You build stronger because you finally know where the cracks were.

Starting over also means releasing the need to explain yourself. Some people will never understand your journey, and that is fine. You are not obligated to convince anyone of your growth. The new you will reveal itself in time. Silence, when rooted in peace, is a sign of confidence.

Starting over is also deeply cultural. In a society like ours, where reputation often feels like currency, it takes courage to begin again publicly. To return to school after others have graduated. To restart a business that people thought had ended. To be known as "the one who started late". But sometimes, being late is divine timing. The wisdom you now have makes you more equipped than you were before. The goal is to start ready, not early.

And readiness is not the absence of fear; it is the decision to move despite it.

There's a Japanese concept called Kintsugi, the art of repairing broken pottery with gold. The cracks are not hidden; they're illuminated. The object becomes more beautiful because it has been broken and restored. That is what starting over does to the human spirit. It turns the cracks into character. It makes you whole in a way perfection never could.

When you rebuild, you begin to understand that the goal is not to become who you were before the fall. It is to become who you couldn't have become without it. You stop asking, Why did this happen to me? And start asking, What is this shaping in me? That is the real anatomy of renewal.

Starting over also requires rest. Not the lazy kind, but the restorative kind. There is a difference between giving up and pausing. The body needs rhythm; so does the soul. If you keep moving without reflecting, you will experience the same fatigue that once broke you. Rest is part of progress.

Over time, your new rhythm becomes your new life. The questions that once haunted you lose their urgency. The people whose opinions once scared you lose their power. You start living again, intentionally, and honestly.

And one day, almost without noticing, you will realise that the new chapter doesn't feel like starting over anymore. It just feels like living.

Starting over is a skill, a way of returning to life again and again, without shame, without fear, and without needing applause.

You rise, you fall, and you rebuild. That is the anatomy of every human story worth telling.

Reflection Section: A Moment to Pause

- What does "starting over" mean to you right now, escape or renewal?
- What patterns from your past have you carried into your new season?
- What small, consistent actions can serve as the foundation for your next chapter?
- What or who must you let go of in order to safeguard your fresh start?
- What cracks in your story could become your gold, your Kintsugi, if you let them?

—Chapter Eleven:—
Learning to Forgive Yourself

"Forgive yourself for not knowing what you didn't know before you learnt it." Maya Angelou

There are some kinds of pain that no apology from the world can fix. The kind that keeps you awake at night, not because someone hurt you, but because you hurt yourself, through neglect, distraction, or delay. The mind can rationalise anything, but the heart remembers what it cost.

The truth about guilt is that it rarely announces its arrival. It begins as a reflection and gradually takes up residence. You start by wanting to learn from your mistakes, but soon you are living in them. It becomes the place you go back to when life becomes uncertain, a kind of emotional habit. Guilt gives you the illusion of control, as though by punishing yourself long enough, you could rewrite what happened. But you cannot. Memory is not a time machine; it is a teacher. It is supposed to instruct, not imprison.

When I think of forgiveness, I think of the work that happens long after everyone else has moved on. The world is quick to tell you to forgive others, but it rarely teaches you how to forgive yourself. We are taught to apologise, to make amends, to let go, but not how to live with the haunting truth that sometimes the person you betrayed most was you.

For me, self-forgiveness was the longest chapter of recovery. Starting over had given me structure; self-forgiveness gave me peace. It required more than effort; it required tenderness, a gentleness I had never been taught to extend inward.

The guilt I carried wasn't only about failing academically. It was about the time I wasted, the opportunities I ignored, and the person I could have been if I had tried harder. I remember sitting alone in my new room at the university, sometimes staring at my notes, sometimes at the ceiling, and thinking, If only I had done this earlier. That phrase, if only, can chain a person more effectively than any external judgement.

Sometimes, what we call guilt is really grief. Grief for the version of ourselves that we lost. The one who believed everything would go right. The one who had simple dreams and unshaken confidence. When that version of yourself vanishes, the pain is not only about what you did wrong but also about the innocence that is lost. Learning to forgive yourself means mourning that version of you, to honour the journey of who you've become.

The truth is, guilt is useful for a moment. It is a teacher when it is fresh. It makes you pause, reflect, and realign. But after it has done its job, it becomes poison. Wallowing in guilt too long turns reflection into rumination. You begin to mistake self-punishment for accountability.

Brené Brown once said that shame corrodes the part of us that believes we can change. That is why forgiveness matters, to protect the part of you that still believes growth is possible. If guilt is the alarm, forgiveness is the reset button. Without it, you'll live in constant noise.

Learning to forgive yourself means learning to see yourself as more than your worst moment. It entails accepting that you are capable of both making mistakes and correcting them. It means speaking to yourself the way you would to a friend who is hurting, with honesty, yes, but also with compassion.

I think of a line from C. S. Lewis: "You can't go back and change the beginning, but you can start where you are and change the ending." It reminded me that regret does not erase the possibility of redemption. You do not need a new beginning to rewrite your story; you only need a new direction.

There were nights I tried to bargain with time, wishing I could relive the years I squandered. But life does not repeat itself for regret; it only repeats lessons for those who refuse to learn them. The mercy of forgiveness is that it allows you to keep your memories without being enslaved by them.

To forgive yourself, you must face the truth without exaggeration. Guilt thrives on distortion. It magnifies what went wrong and shrinks what went right. You begin to think the failure defines the whole story. But if you look closely, even in the mess, there are moments of courage, the times you still tried, and the times you didn't quit. Those details matter. They are evidence of your humanity, not your ruin.

Forgiveness demands proportion. It asks you to see the full picture, not just the corner painted by regret. Sometimes, we overinflate our failures because we need the story to make sense. It feels safer to believe that everything was our fault than to accept that life is partly a mystery. However, self-blame is not wisdom; rather, it is control masquerading as guilt. To truly forgive yourself, you must learn to live with unanswered questions and to make peace with not knowing why some things unfolded the way they did.

One of my favourite lessons in psychology is that the human mind tends to overvalue mistakes and undervalue progress. It is called the "negativity bias". We remember losses more vividly than wins. That is why it feels easier to list your failures than your growth. But what you focus on expands. When you focus on guilt, you nourish despair. When you focus on learning, you nourish resilience.

I had to relearn how to talk to myself. Instead of saying, "I wasted years," I began to say, "I spent years learning what not to do." Instead of saying, "I failed my parents," I said, "I'm learning to make them proud differently." Those small linguistic shifts began to rewire my mindset. The goal was not to deny the past but to narrate it truthfully. Forgiveness begins in how you tell your story back to yourself.

There is a verse in the Qur'an that says, "And do not despair of the mercy of Allah." The emphasis is not on what you have done, but on the mercy that still covers you. Divine mercy, by design, exceeds human guilt. But to experience it, you must stop playing judge and start learning to be a witness. You are no longer in court but in a classroom.

To forgive yourself is to become a student of your mistakes. You do not excuse them; you examine them. You ask, What led me here? What truth was I ignoring? What will I do differently next time? This kind of reflection takes courage. You have to accept looking at your reflection without flinching.

One thing I've learnt is that self-forgiveness doesn't happen in a single moment of enlightenment. It unfolds in layers. You forgive yourself for one thing, then another, then another still. You forgive yourself for what you did and later, for how long it took you to forgive yourself. The process keeps unfolding.

There will be days when you think you've moved on, only for an old regret to tap you on the shoulder. A word, a place, or a familiar date will drag you back to the scene of your mistake. It is easy to panic and think you have undone your progress, but that is not regression; it is part of the process. Healing doesn't forget; it reinterprets. Each return to the memory is another chance to view it through softer eyes. Eventually, the same memory that once bruised you will remind you of how far you've come.

There is a Japanese proverb that says, "Fall seven times, stand up eight." We often quote it as motivation, but it also describes forgiveness. You will fail at forgiving yourself the first few times. The guilt will return. The old voices will whisper. But each time you rise again, it will be with less shame and more strength.

In his book The Road Less Traveled, M. Scott Peck said that self-discipline is self-love in disguise. I think forgiveness is the same. It is not softness; it is stewardship. It is saying, "I will not abandon myself just because I made a mistake." It is refusing to make yourself an enemy.

There is also something cultural about how we carry guilt. Many of us were raised in environments that equated repentance with suffering. If you did not look sad enough, people assumed you hadn't learnt your lesson. But repentance is not supposed to destroy you; it is supposed to restore you. The sign of learning is not perpetual sadness; it is transformation.

The truth is, the person who emerges after forgiveness is

always wiser. They are not as quick to judge others. They listen more. They offer advice gently. They understand that growth requires grace. Forgiving yourself makes you human in a way success never could.

Sometimes, you will have to forgive yourself not for doing wrong, but for not knowing better. You'll look back and realise that the person you were then didn't have the knowledge, the courage, or the clarity you have now. You did what you could with what you had. That realisation doesn't erase responsibility; it redefines it.

As I grew, I realised something simple but profound: you cannot move forward if your energy is invested in self-hate. Bitterness toward yourself is just another form of pride, but forgiveness accepts your humanity. It allows you to live truthfully, even with flaws.

Every time I start a new project, make a new decision, or face a new challenge, I remind myself: you are not the same person who fell. You have learnt, changed, and matured. Self-forgiveness lets you meet life with fresh eyes. Without it, every opportunity becomes a courtroom.

Learning to forgive yourself also means acknowledging that healing doesn't make you immune to mistakes. You will still falter. You will still forget lessons. But you will recover faster because you now know the path back to grace.

When you finally forgive yourself, the world feels lighter. Not because the past disappears, but because it no longer owns you. You walk differently, slower, but freer. You start to love your story again, not as a tragedy but as a testimony.

And that, perhaps, is the real sign of forgiveness: when you can talk about your past without trembling.

You realise that forgiveness was never about changing the past; it was about freeing the future.

Reflection Section: A Moment to Pause

- What part of your story still feels undeserving of compassion?
- In what ways has guilt disguised itself as responsibility in your life?
- What would change if you spoke to yourself with the same kindness you offer others?
- What lessons can your mistakes still teach you if you stop resenting them?
- What would "freedom" look like for you if you finally forgave yourself?

—Chapter Twelve:—
The Purpose Hidden in Pain

"Perhaps you hate a thing, and Allah makes in it much good."
Qur'an 4:19

There are moments in life that tear through you so deeply that words become useless. You do not want advice. You do not want pity. You just want to understand why. Why this loss, why this delay, why this disappointment that feels like betrayal? For a long time, I used to believe pain was a punishment, and that when life hurt, it meant I had done something wrong.

But with time, I have learnt that pain is not always a verdict. Sometimes, it is an invitation. It doesn't always come to destroy you; sometimes, it comes to direct you.

Pain interrupts patterns we would never have broken by choice. It pauses our routines and asks the questions we keep postponing: Is this the life you want? Is this the person you are becoming? Most of us only change when comfort becomes unbearable. Pain, in that sense, is clarity disguised as discomfort. It breaks what was built on illusion so that truth can breathe again.

I thought my life was over when I fell. What I didn't see then was that I was being refined. Pain stripped away the illusions I had built around myself: the illusion of control, of self-sufficiency, of untested strength. It revealed what I truly valued and what I only claimed to value. It was, in a strange way, the most honest teacher I'd ever had.

In Man's Search for Meaning, Viktor Frankl wrote that suffering ceases to be suffering at the moment it finds meaning. I didn't understand that sentence when I first read it. But I do now. Pain without purpose feels like chaos. Pain with purpose becomes formation. When you can connect your pain to something larger, like growth, wisdom, or empathy, it begins to hurt differently. It doesn't stop hurting, but it stops being senseless.

Pain changes you, but the choice of how it changes you is yours. It can make you bitter or tender. It can close your heart or open it wider. It can leave you fearful or make you fearless. Pain never leaves you neutral; it leaves you transformed.

Yet, transformation is not instant. It happens slowly, like dawn, so gradual that you often mistake progress for stillness. You think nothing is changing until one day you wake up to find your perception altered, your reactions calmer, and your gratitude deeper. This is how pain does its work.

When you are in the middle of it, though, nothing about it feels meaningful. Pain doesn't reveal its purpose immediately. It is only in hindsight that you see how it was shaping you. The sleepless nights, the unanswered prayers, and the detours all look random until one day you realise they were rearranging your life in necessary ways.

Khalil Gibran, in The Prophet, wrote, "Your pain is the breaking of the shell that encloses your understanding." Pain cracks the shell of comfort that keeps you from depth. It forces you to see, listen, and feel differently. It teaches you that wisdom does not come from winning; it comes from enduring.

I remember one night in particular, a night that felt endless. I couldn't sleep; my mind was racing, and everything I had been running from came crashing in at once. I realised how afraid I was of not becoming who I wanted to be. That fear hurt more than any failure. But in that moment, something profound happened. I stopped resisting. I sat in the pain and just breathed. For the first time, I tried to process everything. And in that stillness, I began to sense something new, almost like surrender.

That was the night I learnt that pain can be sacred when it pushes you closer to truth.

Everyone, in my opinion, eventually reaches a point where all they can do is give up. That surrender is not weakness; it is alignment. It is the realisation that healing comes from allowing your pain to teach you. When you stop demanding that life be painless, you begin to grow from within it.

Rumi wrote, "The wound is the place where the Light enters you." I used to think that was just poetry. But I have come to see that it is not a metaphor; it is a fact. Wounds make space. They carve room for empathy, humility, and depth. Without pain, you remain shallow. Without wounds, you never develop the kind of sight that can see beauty in broken things.

Every person I admire has been through something that broke them. It is as if greatness requires wounding. The artists, thinkers, and spiritual leaders all met pain and learnt to translate it. They mastered the language of loss and used it to create something that outlived them.

But you do not have to be extraordinary to learn that lesson.

Pain is democratic; it reaches everyone. What differs is what we do with it. Some people let pain close their hearts. Others permit it to open their eyes.

For a long time, I let pain define me. I spoke about it as if it were my identity. "This is who I am, the one who failed." But slowly, I began to realise that pain wasn't who I was; it was what I had been through. It was a teacher, not a title. Once I separated the two, I could finally breathe again.

Breathing again after pain feels unfamiliar at first. You have been holding your breath for so long that peace almost feels undeserved. You wait for another disappointment, another wave of loss. But healing is learning to trust joy again and believing that you can feel light without fearing what follows. The ability to rest in peace after pain is itself a sign of transformation.

Pain also reveals the fragility of pride. It humbles you. It teaches you how dependent you truly are on time, on others, and on God. You realise how small you are and yet how deeply you are seen. Remember the verse in the Qur'an that says, "Indeed, with hardship comes ease"? Notice that it doesn't say after hardship, but with it. Meaning is born in the middle of the storm, not after it has passed.

It's difficult to accept that when you are suffering. You think ease will only come when the pain ends. But more often than not, ease comes as perspective, not escape. It comes as understanding that pain, too, is part of your story and not a detour from it.

Perspective is not denial. It doesn't erase the memory of pain; it simply rearranges its meaning. You begin to see that the things you lost were never random; they created room for what you now hold. What left was not wasted; it made space for what is growing. This is the arithmetic of divine mercy: subtraction before multiplication.

I have learnt to stop asking, Why is this happening to me? And start asking, What is this teaching me? That one shift turns failure into a classroom. It turns despair into dialogue.

Sometimes, pain teaches you to slow down. To let go of control. To see people. To appreciate the small moments of life. It teaches gratitude by subtraction, by showing you how fragile joy is and how much of it you took for granted.

Pain also introduces you to parts of yourself that comfort never could. It reveals your limits, yes, but also your resilience. It reveals how much strength was hiding beneath your fear. It forces you to live with intention because now you know that peace is not permanent and time is not guaranteed.

Comfort protects us; pain perfects us. The former maintains what is, while the latter reveals what can be. In comfort, you learn pleasure; in pain, you learn perspective. And between both, life balances its curriculum. You cannot graduate from one without attending the other. The secret is not to idolise either season but to learn to move gracefully through both.

In The Road to Character, David Brooks wrote that suffering carves deep grooves in the soul that later allow for joy. He stated that those who have suffered greatly tend to live with a sense of moral depth, seriousness about life, and tenderness for others. I see it in those who have rebuilt themselves. Pain has sharpened their perception.

Every time I reflect on my pain, I realise it was never wasted. Every delay, every rejection, every heartbreak they were all

doing invisible work. They were strengthening muscles I didn't know I had: patience, empathy, and endurance. They were shaping me into someone who could carry both success and sorrow without collapsing.
There is an African proverb that says, "The child who is not embraced by the village will burn it down to feel its warmth." It reminds me that unhealed pain doesn't disappear. If you do not transform your pain, you transmit it to others, to relationships, and to the next version of yourself. It is forgiveness and reflection that turn pain from a weapon into wisdom.

You have to allow your pain to heal properly if you want to find meaning in it. Do not rush to label it. Do not romanticise it either. Sit with it long enough to let it reveal its message. The point is not to justify suffering but to draw meaning from it.

When I look back now, I no longer resent what I went through. The pain that once felt like punishment became the soil for everything that grew afterwards. It broke me open in ways that ambition never could. It taught me how to value people, how to slow down, and how to pray differently. It showed me that mercy can sometimes take the form of disguise.

Looking back, I realise that every version of me that emerged after pain was more grounded, more patient, and more aware. It is as though pain peeled away the noise, leaving only the essential. It didn't just change my life; it changed the way I lived it. The things I once chased for validation lost their shine, replaced by meaningful pursuits meaning, gratitude, and depth. That is the ultimate mercy of pain: it teaches you to measure life differently.

The purpose hidden in pain is never found through analysis alone. It is found through surrender. You do not always have to understand the "why". You only need to trust that the "why" exists. When you do not get answers, that trust is what keeps you going.

One day, you will look back and realise that your pain gave you language. It made you fluent in compassion. It gave you stories that could heal others. It gave you eyes that can recognise strength in silence.

And perhaps that is why pain exists at all, to remind us that we are fragile, yet unbreakable. To remind us that growth is not found in avoidance but in awareness. To teach us that even in darkness, purpose is being written.

Pain doesn't mean God is absent. Sometimes, it means He is too close for comfort, chiselling away what no longer serves you, refining your patience, and teaching you to depend on something higher than control.

The next time life hurts, resist the urge to escape it too quickly. Ask instead: What is this pain protecting me from? What is it preparing me for? What strength is it revealing in me?

Pain may not always answer, but it always shapes.
And if you allow it, pain will build you into someone who can walk through fire and still carry light.

Reflection Section: A Moment to Pause

- What pain in your life are you still interpreting as punishment rather than preparation?
- What has your suffering taught you that peace never could?
- How might your wounds be creating space for new understanding or empathy?
- In what ways has pain humbled you into clarity or dependence on God?
- What purpose might your current discomfort be serving, even if you can't see it yet?

—Chapter Thirteen:— You Can Begin Again

"The greatest glory in living lies not in never falling, but in rising every time we fall." Nelson Mandela

Every story that breaks has the power to begin again. That is the miracle of being human, that no matter how far you have drifted, you are never beyond return.

For a long time, I thought beginnings were reserved for the young, the lucky, or the unbroken. I thought starting over was a privilege of those who had managed to keep their lives intact. But I have learnt that beginnings are not given; they are chosen. They happen when you decide that your last chapter will not be your last chance.

You can begin again, not because you have solved everything, but because you have survived enough to know what matters. You can start over because growth doesn't expire.

Most of us wait for some external confirmation before starting again a sign, a person's approval, or a perfect condition. But beginnings rarely arrive with permission slips. They meet you halfway, responding only to movement. When you take the first trembling step, the path reveals itself step by step.

The phrase "begin again" sounds simple, but it is an act of rebellion. It means standing in the middle of the same place that once saw your fall and saying, "I am not finished here." It means refusing to let a single version of your story define the entire book.

When I look back now, I see that my journey didn't restart the day I got another admission. It started the day I stopped running from my reflection. That was the real beginning, the day I chose to see myself not as a failure, but as a student of failure.

Being a student of failure changes how you carry yourself. You no longer chase perfection; you chase comprehension. Every mistake becomes a lesson plan, every setback a field study. Failure stops being a verdict and becomes a curriculum. That mindset makes beginning again less frightening because you've already learnt how to learn.

There is a passage by Mary Oliver where she asks, "Tell me, what is it you plan to do with your one wild and precious life?" I used to read that as a question about ambition. Now I read it as a question about renewal. Life becomes precious when you realise how fragile and fleeting it is.

The truth is, beginning again is not always about doing more. Sometimes, it is about doing less but doing it from a clearer place. It is about simplifying your desires, shedding your expectations, and learning to live from the inside out. Renewal is not addition; it is subtraction until only what is essential remains.

In a world that glorifies the accumulation of titles and possessions, it takes courage to subtract. To choose simplicity in a noisy age is an act of rebellion. When you start again, you learn that peace doesn't come from having more but from needing less. What remains after you simplify is usually what was meant to be there all along.

When you choose to begin again, you reclaim authorship of your life. You stop letting fear write your script. You stop letting regret dictate your tone. You take back the pen, knowing that every line you write from here will carry the wisdom of all that came before.

Sometimes, that wisdom shows up as humility. You stop trying to control every outcome because you have learnt that peace and perfection do not live in the same house. You learn to hold your plans lightly and your faith tightly.

Faith is not the absence of doubt; it is the courage to move while doubting. It is the steady conviction that there is something sacred about persistence. You can begin again, not because the path is clear, but because the direction is right.

Allah said in the Qur'an, "And whoever puts his trust in Allah, He will suffice him." Trust is not passive; it is an active surrender. It means doing your part while releasing the illusion of control. It is the recognition that detours can sometimes be divine routes.

To begin again, you must first forgive yourself for the time you lost. You must stop treating delay as a disqualification. The pace of your journey is not evidence of your worth. Sometimes, God slows you down to save you from becoming someone you are not ready to be.

Delay is not denial; it is divine pacing. The pause between what you want and when it comes is often where strength is built. Every detour has a hidden design of preparing character for capacity. When you see delay as training, you stop despising it. You begin to understand that time can be a teacher, not an enemy.

Beginnings are not always glamorous. Most of the time, they are subtle decisions made in the privacy of your heart. They simply grow roots until one day, you wake up different and more determined.

I've come to believe that everyone who falls receives two gifts: a new perspective and a choice. Perspective reveals what truly matters; choice determines what comes next. You can remain in regret, or you can rise in gratitude. Both are valid, but only one moves you forward.

It took me years to understand that redemption is not about erasing the past. It is about transforming its meaning. When I look at my old self now, the scared, uncertain version who thought failure was final, I do not feel shame anymore. I feel gratitude because that version of me endured what I now teach from.

In The Value of Failure, Shane Lester writes, "Failure is not the opposite of progress; it is the process through which integrity is tested and strengthened. Each fall invites us to confront our illusions, not so that we can avoid falling again, but so that we can fall better next time." His words reveal the deeper truth about renewal: that growth is not born from victory but from honesty. The goal is not to avoid failure but to learn how to fall with awareness, rise with humility, and continue without resentment. Every fall refines integrity; every rise refines purpose.

The day you begin again is not when everything becomes easy. It is when you decide to live differently and to believe that your life still carries purpose even when it has been interrupted.

Rising again doesn't always mean upward motion. Sometimes, it is inward, learning to sit with yourself without shame, learning to stay when it gets hard, and learning to love what's still unfinished. Every time you choose compassion over condemnation, you are rising. Every time you silence the voice that says you're too late, you are beginning again.

The inward rise is the hardest to measure because it doesn't show on paper. There are no certificates for inner peace, no applause for healing. Yet these invisible victories are the ones that sustain every visible one. The calm you build within becomes the foundation for whatever comes next.

In The Book of Awakening, Mark Nepo wrote, "When we face what we fear, we become intimate with life." That is what starting over feels like: intimacy with life. You stop trying to survive and start living honestly.

Beginning again doesn't mean pretending the fall never happened. It means walking with the memory but without the weight. It means learning from the pain without being consumed by it. It means letting your scars speak of where you have been, not of what you have lost.

There is something freeing about realising that you are not who you used to be. You do not need to keep proving you have changed; just live like it. Time will testify.

Sometimes, the most spiritual act you can perform is simply trying again. You send another application. You show up to another class. You believe in love again. You trust that effort still matters.

In a world obsessed with finality, beginnings are acts of faith. They say, "I still believe in growth, in mercy, and in tomorrow."

The real victory is refusing to let any fall define you. Your worth was never dependent on your performance. It was written before you ever began, and it remains intact even when you stumble.

So if today feels heavy, if you feel behind, if old mistakes haunt you, pause. Breathe. This, too, can be your beginning. Because the truth is, no matter how far you've gone, grace always knows the way back.

And every sunrise is God's reminder that you can begin again.

Somewhere, a version of you is still waiting for proof that redemption is real. Let this be it. Every breath you take is evidence that God kept you here for a reason. You do not need a sign louder than survival itself. The sunrise is not a coincidence; it is a continuation.

Reflection Section: A Moment to Pause

- What might beginning again look like for you, in mindset?
- What fear has been convincing you that your story is over?
- What new rhythm or value are you being invited to embody right now?
- Who could you become if you stopped apologising for where you've been?
- What small step could you take today that says, clearly, I am beginning again?

Epilogue

There is a moment after every storm when the sky feels confused. The clouds are still heavy, the air is still unsettled, but light begins to leak through in small ways. This is just to tell you that darkness cannot stay forever.

This book was born in that kind of light.

I did not write these pages as someone who conquered life. I wrote them as someone who was broken in full view of the world and still found a reason to rise. My failure, like every other, just happened suddenly, painfully, and without mercy. But my healing came with choice. It came slowly. It came gently. It came in moments that looked ordinary but carried God's fingerprints.

If there is anything my story has taught me, it is that falling is not the end of a life. It is a clarion call to meet the parts of yourself you abandoned when everything was going well. You learn what you truly believe. You learn who truly stays. You learn how to sit with yourself without fear. You learn that God does not step back when you crumble. He steps closer.

Many of us wait for a grand turning point. We imagine a day when everything aligns. But becoming again rarely happens in a single moment. It takes a lot of effort and sincere conversations and strong-willed decisions. It happens when you choose honesty over shame. It happens when you forgive yourself for the first time. It happens when you wake up and try again even though fear is louder than courage.

You may not feel ready to rebuild. You may still see pieces of your old life scattered everywhere. You may feel like you have disappointed yourself, your family, and your Creator. But even that feeling is not the end. It is the doorway. It is the proof that your soul is still alive enough to want better.

Your story is not ruined. It is unfolding.

If you are reading this with a heart that feels tired, I want you to know something I learnt on the night I walked around my campus overwhelmed with regret: it is possible to start again without shame. It is possible to rise even if you broke yourself. It is possible to grow even if you once walked in the wrong direction. Nothing about your past disqualifies you from a future that has been written with mercy.

The truth is simple. You do not become again by pretending you never fell. You become again by collecting your pieces, placing them in the hands of God, and allowing His mercy to remake you. You become again by choosing to believe that your life can hold beauty after disappointment. You become again by stepping into the next chapter, even if your legs are shaking.

And one day, without noticing when it happened, you will see that you have grown tall in places you once felt small. You will breathe differently. You will walk differently. You will carry your own name with tenderness instead of shame.

This is not the end of my story. It is not the end of yours either.

It is only a reminder that beginnings do not end with failure.
They wait for you inside it.

So here is my last call to you.
Stand up gently.
Return to yourself slowly.
Let God meet you where you are.
And when you feel ready, even if you do not feel brave, choose to begin again.

Your becoming has only just started.

About the Author

Abdulbasit Abdusalam is a Nigerian writer, communications strategist, and founder of InkVision Creatives, a writing and executive communications studio. Through his studio, he has worked with professionals across diverse sectors, crafting narratives that strengthen personal brands, enhance career mobility, and communicate expertise with depth and clarity. His approach blends journalistic precision with empathetic storytelling, making his work both intellectually grounded and emotionally resonant.

A graduate of Lagos State University, Abdulbasit's journey was shaped by an early academic setback that sparked a season of reflection and reinvention. That experience now fuels his commitment to guiding others through failure, rediscovery, and purposeful growth.

He is passionate about faith-rooted resilience, personal development, and empowering young adults to rebuild their lives with intention and renewed confidence. His debut book, Becoming Again, reflects this mission.